# UKRAINE
## in Pictures

**VGS**

Jeffrey Zuehlke

Lerner Publications Company

# Contents

Lerner Publications Company
A division of Lerner Publishing Group
241 First Avenue North
Minneapolis, MN 55401 U.S.A.

Website address: www.lernerbooks.com

web enhanced @ www.vgsbooks.com

Library of Congress Cataloging-in-Publication Data

Zuehlke, Jeffrey, 1968–
     Ukraine in pictures / by Jeffrey Zuehlke.
        p.   cm. — (Visual geography series)
     Includes bibliographical references and index.
     ISBN-13: 978-0-8225-2398-7 (lib. bdg. : alk. paper)
     ISBN-10: 0-8225-2398-1 (lib. bdg. : alk. paper)
        1. Ukraine—Juvenile literature. 2. Ukraine—Pictorial works—Juvenile literature. I. Title. II. Series:
Visual geography series (Minneapolis, Minn.)
DK508.12.Z84 2006
947.7'0022'2—dc22                                                         2004022724

Manufactured in the United States of America
1 2 3 4 5 6 – BP – 11 10 09 08 07 06

# INTRODUCTION

Late in 2004, the eastern European nation of Ukraine made headlines around the world. After a bitterly contested campaign, two presidential candidates, Viktor Yushchenko and Prime Minister Viktor Yanukovych, faced off in an election on November 21. Shortly after the polls closed, Yanukovych was declared the winner. Yet election monitors, both Ukrainians as well as observers from the United States and Europe, declared the election unfair. They claimed that voter intimidation, ballot box stuffing, and voter fraud had been performed in favor of Yanukovych.

In response, thousands of Yushchenko supporters flooded the frozen streets of the Ukrainian capital, Kyiv (spelled Kiev in Russian), to protest the election results. For weeks the protesters blocked the entrances to government buildings, effectively shutting down government operations. As journalists from around the world traveled to Ukraine to cover these extraordinary events, governments around the world—including the U.S. government—sided with the protesters in condemning the elections as unfair.

In the weeks that followed, more extraordinary events occurred. On December 1, Ukraine's parliament (legislative body) passed a vote of no confidence, which automatically triggered the resignation of Prime Minister Yanukovych's government. (Yanukovych refused to accept this ruling and remained in office.) Days later, the Supreme Court declared the election result void and called for a new election. Parliament then adopted new election rules in hopes of creating a more fair election.

On December 26, voters returned to the polls, giving Yushchenko a decisive victory. The dramatic events highlighted many of the challenges facing Ukraine, a country that has been independent only since 1991, when it broke away from the disintegrating Union of Soviet Socialist Republics (USSR). The candidates' opposing views in many ways mirror the regions from which they draw support. Yushchenko is widely seen as pro-Western. He believes that Ukraine's future will be brightest through more trade and contact with the West, including Europe and the United States. Many of Yushchenko's supporters live in

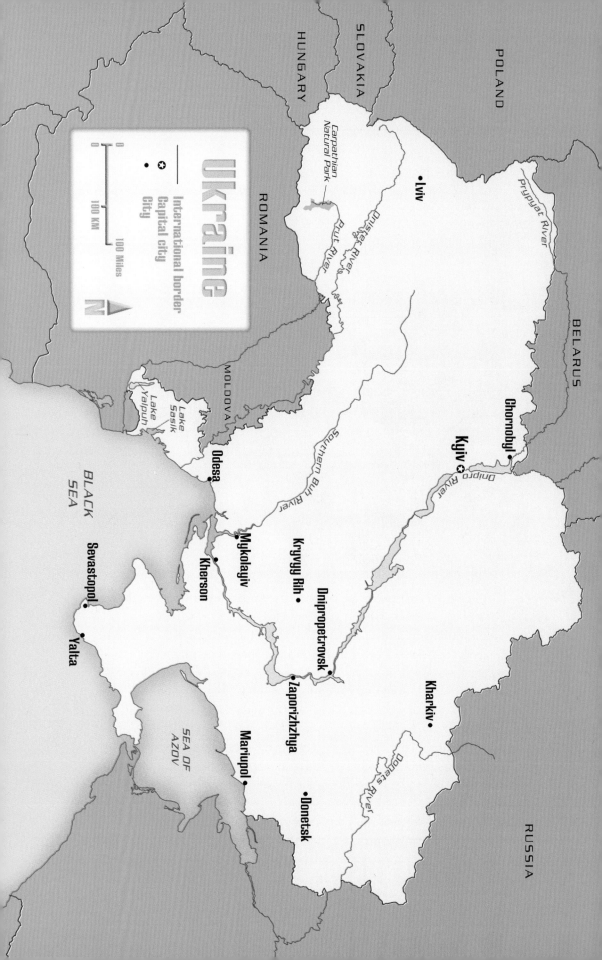

the western part of Ukraine, where ties to Europe are stronger than in the east. The pro-Russian Yanukovych received strong support in the pro-Russian stronghold of eastern Ukraine.

Controversy and division are nothing new in Ukraine, a land that has served as a battleground for internal and external powers since ancient times. Lying at the crossroads between Europe, Asia, and the Middle East, Ukraine was a prize that tempted a succession of outside invaders. Consisting of mostly flat, fertile plains, Ukraine has virtually no natural borders to provide defense. As a result, the region has changed hands numerous times and suffered greatly under foreign rulers.

Since becoming an independent nation in 1991, Ukrainians are changing the spellings of their cities and regions from Russian back to Ukrainian. For example, the Russian spelling of the capital city, Kiev, is slowly being replaced by the Ukrainian spelling, Kyiv. For this book, Ukrainian spellings have been used whenever available, with Russian spelling followed in parentheses.

Ukraine's suffering reached its peak in the twentieth century. As part of the crumbling Russian Empire, the country was a battleground first in World War I (1914–1918) and then in the Russian Civil War (1918–1920). When these wars ended, hundreds of thousands of Ukrainians were dead, and hopes for Ukrainian independence were dashed. Ukraine remained under the control of Russia, this time as part of the Soviet Union (1922–1991). Then, in the late 1920s and early 1930s, Soviet leader Joseph Stalin sought to break the independent spirit of Ukraine once and for all by setting into motion a massive famine that led to the death of millions of Ukrainians. A few years later, German troops invaded Ukraine, and the country became a battleground once again, this time in the most costly war in history, World War II (1939–1945).

Throughout Soviet rule, Ukraine was the breadbasket and industrial center of the Soviet economy. Ukrainian hopes of independence were muted until the 1980s, when the Soviet government weakened. Outraged by their government's careless handling of the deadly 1986 explosion at the Chornobyl (Chernobyl) nuclear power plant in northern Ukraine, Ukrainians seized their opportunity to speak out, setting in motion a chain of events that resulted in a vote for independence in 1991.

Ukraine has struggled since becoming an independent nation. But with abundant natural resources and some of the world's most fertile farmland, the country has an opportunity to achieve great prosperity. And Ukrainians' bold response to the political events of 2004 have shown that the country has a spirit that will not be broken.

# THE LAND

Ukraine lies north of the Black Sea in southeastern Europe. With an area of 233,089 square miles (603,700 square kilometers), the country is the second largest in Europe (after Russia) and the largest country completely within Europe. Ukraine is slightly smaller than the state of Texas. Romania and the former Soviet republic of Moldova lie southwest of Ukraine. Hungary and Slovakia share short frontiers to the west. Belarus and Poland lie to the north and northwest, respectively. Ukraine's long eastern border with Russia runs from Belarus southward to the Sea of Azov, an arm of the Black Sea.

The name Ukraine comes from a Slavic word meaning "borderland." Throughout its history, Ukraine has been a gateway for travelers moving eastward to Asia, as well as an important route westward into Europe. The region also formed the westernmost territory of the historic Russian Empire. Although newly independent, Ukraine remains closely tied to Russia and to the eastern European nations that have, at various times, claimed Ukrainian lands and influenced Ukrainian culture.

## Topography

Most of Ukraine's territory is made up of level, fertile plains—known as steppes—that are similar to the Great Plains that stretch across most of the central United States. Elevations on the steppes are greatest in the north and west and gradually decrease near the coast of the Black Sea.

Ukraine is generally divided into six geographical regions. The Carpathian Mountains cut across the country's western corner. This region is among Ukraine's most picturesque and is home to Mount Hoverla, the highest point in the country at 6,762 feet (2,061 meters).

In northern Ukraine lie the Dnipro-Prypyat Lowlands, which are named after two rivers that flow through the region. Once almost completely forested, the land has been cleared as a result of extensive logging. Another feature of this lowland region is the sandy Prypyat Marshes, the largest area of marshland in Europe. Crossed by many river valleys, the marshes are sparsley settled, although some of the

For much of its history, Ukraine was known as *the* Ukraine, because it was considered to be simply an extension of the larger Russian (and later Soviet) Empire. After Ukraine became an independent nation, the government announced that the nation would be known as Ukraine to distinguish it as a separate country.

land has been drained for use as grazing land for cattle.

Northeastern Ukraine is the country's most heavily populated area. It is made up of a low plateau known as the Northern Ukrainian Upland. This farming area produces grains and sugar beets (Ukraine's most important crops) and rests upon large deposits of natural gas. The Central Plateau, Ukraine's largest geographical region, stretches across the middle of the country. Its rich, black soil, called *chornozem,* is some of the most fertile in the world and makes Ukraine one of the world's most productive agricultural nations.

The Coastal Plain lies south of the Central Plateau and includes most of the Crimean Peninsula, a mass of land that juts into the Black Sea. The plain receives little rainfall and is sometimes referred to as desert steppe. Farmers in this region often rely on irrigation to water their crops. Ukraine's lowest point—sea level along the coast of the Black Sea—is located on the Coastal Plain.

The Crimean Mountains run along the southern shore of the Crimean Peninsula. The peninsula, often referred to as simply the Crimea, is popular with tourists, who flock to its sandy Black Sea beaches. Farmers also cultivate the hillsides, where vineyards, as well as cherry and apple orchards, thrive.

## Rivers and Lakes

Four major rivers—the Dnipro (Dnieper), Dnister (Dniester), Southern Buh (Southurn Bug), and Donets—flow through Ukraine. The wide Dnipro River crosses into Ukraine from Belarus. It winds for 609 miles (980 kilometers) through Ukraine's broad, flat plains before reaching its outlet into the Black Sea near the southern city of Kherson. In central and southern Ukraine, the Dnipro flows through dams that generate hydroelectric power. These dams have also created several large reservoirs (artificial lakes). The Dnipro has been one of Europe's most important trading routes for centuries and remains so in modern times.

The Dnister is Ukraine's second-longest river. It begins in the Carpathian Mountains in the west, flows in a southeasterly direction through Moldova, then cuts again through Ukraine before draining into the Black Sea. The Southern Buh River also begins in the west.

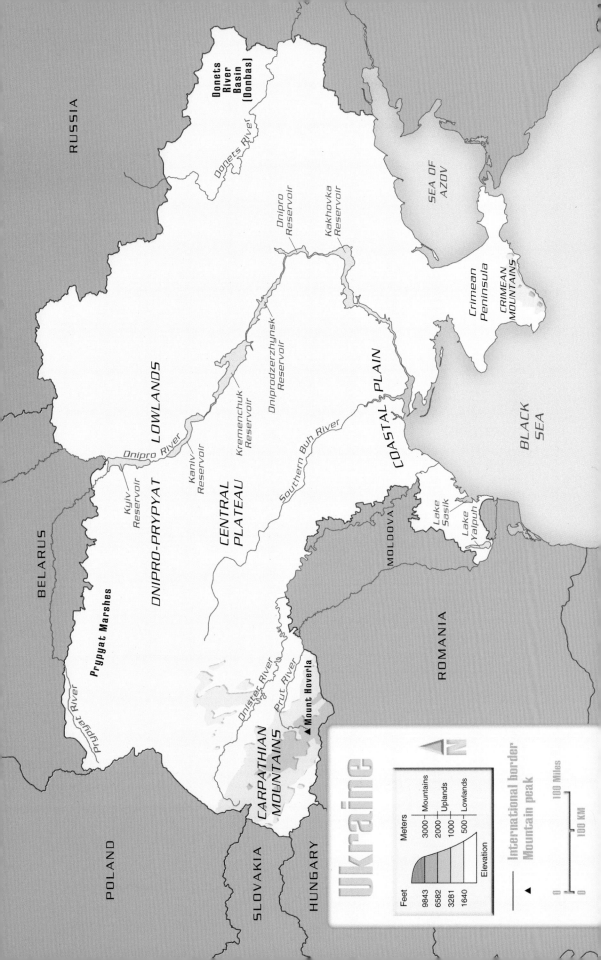

# Ukraine

RUSSIA

BELARUS

POLAND

SLOVAKIA

HUNGARY

MOLDOVA

ROMANIA

**Donets River Basin (Donbas)**

*Donets River*

SEA OF AZOV

*Dnipro Reservoir*

*Kakhovka Reservoir*

Crimean Peninsula

CRIMEAN MOUNTAINS

DNIPRO-PRYPYAT LOWLANDS

*Dnipro River*

*Dniprodzerzhynsk Reservoir*

*Kremenchuk Reservoir*

COASTAL PLAIN

*Kaniv Reservoir*

*Kyiv Reservoir*

CENTRAL PLATEAU

*Southern Buh River*

**Prypyat Marshes**

*Prypyat River*

*Dnister River*

*Prut River*

▲ Mount Hoverla

CARPATHIAN MOUNTAINS

Lake Sasik

Lake Yalpuh

BLACK SEA

N

Elevation

| Feet | Meters | |
|---|---|---|
| 9843 | 3000 | Mountains |
| 6582 | 2000 | Uplands |
| 3281 | 1000 | |
| 1640 | 500 | Lowlands |

—— International border
▲ Mountain peak

0    100 Miles
0    100 KM

A train crosses a bridge over **the Dnipro River.** The Dnipro is Europe's fourth-longest river, winding for 1,420 miles (2,285 km). Half of Ukraine's other rivers drain into the Dnipro.

The country's third-longest river runs for 532 miles (856 km) through central Ukraine before draining into the Black Sea. The upper part of the Southern Buh has many rapids, which make navigation impossible but provide a good source of hydroelectric power for the region.

The Donets begins in Russia and flows through the eastern part of Ukraine before reentering Russia. The Donets cuts through an area known as the Donets River basin (commonly referred to as the Donbas), a center for Ukraine's mining and industry. Exploitation of the basin's coal and iron reserves have caused extensive pollution and environmental damage, and the Donets is one of Europe's most polluted rivers.

Ukraine's largest lakes are the reservoirs—the Kyiv, the Kaniv, the Kremenchuk, the Dniprodzerzhynsk, the Dnipro, and the Kakhovka—created by the damming of the Dnipro River. Water from these lakes is used for irrigation and for drinking water. Ukraine is home to natural bodies of both salt water and freshwater. The largest saltwater lake is Lake Sasik, which covers 79 square miles (205 sq. km) on the Crimean Peninsula. Lake Yalpuh, in the far southwest, is Ukraine's largest freshwater lake (58 square miles or 150 sq. km).

## Climate

Most of Ukraine experiences warm summers and cold winters. Average January temperatures range from 28°F (–2°C) in the southwest to 18°F (–8°C) in the northeast. Kyiv averages 21°F (–6°C) in January, the coldest month, and 67°F (19°C) in July, the warmest month. Throughout most of the country, snow covers the ground for about three months during the winter.

Rainfall during the summer is heaviest in the northwest, where the average annual precipitation is 24 inches (61 centimeters). More than 31 inches (80 cm) of rain and snow fall in the Carpathian Mountains.

Summer storms interrupt long periods of warm and dry weather throughout the country. July temperatures average about 70°F (21°C). Hot, dry winds known as *sukhoviyi* blow from the east in the summer, causing occasional droughts. With moderate temperatures and precipitation, autumn and spring in southern Ukraine are longer than in steppe regions to the north and east. The Crimea enjoys dry, hot summers and mild winters.

## Flora and Fauna

Ukraine's forests, steppes, mountains, and streams are home to about 16,000 kinds of plants and 28,000 species of animals. Nearly 16 percent of the country is forested, with most of the woodlands found in the north and west. A wide variety of trees—including alder, aspen, beech, birch, elm, fir, hornbeam, linden, maple, oak, pine, and spruce—grow in these regions. The Prypyat Marshes of the northwest are home to a variety of reeds and grasses, such as cattails, cotton grass, and reed grass.

Ukraine's other forests are located in the Carpathian and Crimean mountains, where fir, spruce, and sycamore trees grow. Other mountain plants include grasses and low-growing flowers, such as edelweiss, a rare, star-shaped flower with white petals, which Ukrainians call the magic silk flower.

**Edelweiss**

Flowers are also found in abundance on the steppe. They include crocuses, forget-me-nots, irises, hyacinths, sunflowers, poppies, bachelor's buttons, and tulips. A wide variety of grasses also grow here, along with occasional small stands of oak, elm, and willow trees.

The steppe is home to many different kinds of animals. One of the best-known Ukrainian mammals is the marmot, a large rodent from the squirrel family that burrows and inhabits underground tunnels. Marmots live in colonies and have developed an effective system of protection against predators. Members of the colony stand guard outside of the burrow and make a very loud and piercing shriek when predators approach. Mammals such as wolves, roe deer, and wild pigs live in the mountains.

Ukrainian birds include golden eagles, short-toed eagles, red-capped woodpeckers, and kingfishers. Grouse, owls, gulls, and partridges also thrive in Ukraine. Fish, such as pike, carp, perch, and sturgeon are found in the country's lakes and rivers, although overfishing in past decades has severely limited their numbers.

## Natural Resources and Environmental Concerns

Ukraine's abundant natural resources attracted outside powers to conquer the region at various periods in its history. In addition to vast areas of fertile farmland (57 percent of the country is suitable for farming), Ukraine also has extensive reserves of iron ore, coal, manganese (used in the production of steel), natural gas, oil, salt, sulfur, graphite, titanium, magnesium, kaolin (a soft white clay used in making china, porcelain, paper, rubber, paint, and many other products), nickel, and mercury.

However, this wealth of resources has been exploited, often to disastrous effect. Soviet leaders, determined to rapidly industrialize the Soviet Union, paid little attention to the devastating environmental damage caused to Ukraine by reckless mining techniques, water pollution, air pollution, and rapid deforestation. Such practices and their harmful effects helped to inspire the country's population in its move toward independence in the 1980s.

Air and water quality are poor in much of Ukraine, particularly in the industrial cities Zaporizhzhya and Kryvyy Rih. Destructive deforestation practices led to the country's worst natural disaster in 1998, when floods and landslides—made worse by a lack of trees and plants to keep soil in place—destroyed hundreds of roads, dams, bridges, buildings, and homes in the western part of the country. Thousands of Ukrainians were left homeless.

Yet Ukraine's most costly environmental disaster was the 1986 explosion at the Chornobyl nuclear power plant, which contaminated a

A team of scientists tests for radiation over the demolished **nuclear reactor at Chornobyl.** In 1986 an explosion at the Chornobyl nuclear power plant spread deadly radioactive material across Ukraine and Belarus. For links to more information about the disaster at Chornobyl, visit www.vgsbooks.com.

large swath of northern Ukraine and neighboring Belarus with deadly radioactive material. Decades after the event, the country is still coping with its effects. Since the disaster, Ukrainians have held protests against nuclear power plants. Because of these efforts, some completed reactors have never opened, and others in the planning stages have never been built. Nevertheless, reactors at Chornobyl that were not damaged by the explosion remained in operation for more than a decade until the plant was finally closed down completely in 2000.

## Cities

About two-thirds of Ukraine's 48.1 million people live in cities. The country has several urban centers with more than 1 million residents and many medium-sized towns. Kyiv, the Ukrainian capital, is a city of 2.6 million people on the Dnipro River in the north central part of the country. The city's legendary founder, the seventh-century ruler Kyi, built a fortress to protect the site from raids by the nomads of the steppes. Later, Kyiv became a major trading center that linked the Black Sea region with nations and cities in northern Europe.

Kyiv was the seat of the earliest Slavic principalities (states ruled by princes), as well as an important religious hub. The Tatars of central Asia overran and destroyed the city in the thirteenth century. Kyiv became a possession of the kingdom of Lithuania in the fourteenth century, after the Tatars retreated from eastern Europe. The city was brought into the Russian Empire in the 1600s. During World War II, fighting between German and Soviet

## THE CHORNOBYL EXPLOSION

On April 26, 1986, an experiment performed by engineers at one of the reactors at the Chornobyl nuclear power plant in northern Ukraine caused an explosion. The blast started more than thirty fires and threw 11 tons (10 metric tons) of radioactive particles into the air. The radiation (high-energy rays) destroys living tissue, causing cancer, birth defects, or even death in people, animals, and plants.

The increased radiation in the area has caused thousands of people to suffer from cancer, blood diseases, and stomach ailments. Chornobyl itself is a ghost town. Cleanup crews bulldozed and buried houses and trees beneath the contaminated soil. Workers enclosed the destroyed reactor in steel and cement, but radiation continues to leak. Most experts doubt that people will ever be able to live safely in Chornobyl again, and many believe that the consequences of the explosion will still be evident for thousands of years.

**Historic buildings in the Ukrainian capital of Kyiv undergo restoration.** Many of Ukraine's cities have undergone extensive reconstruction since independence.

forces caused extensive destruction in the city. Nevertheless, many of Kyiv's historic churches and public buildings have survived.

Kyiv remains an important industrial center and provides a vital transportation hub for Ukraine's farms and factories. Workers in the city's factories produce cameras, precision tools, clothing, aircraft, watches, and chemicals.

East of Kyiv is Kharkiv (Kharkov—population 1.5 million), a city settled by the military brotherhood of Cossacks in the seventeenth century. Located near vast fields of coal and iron ore, Kharkiv has become the country's chief industrial city. In addition, it is a lively cultural and literary hub with a long tradition of music, theater, and opera.

An important industrial city along the Dnipro River is Dnipropetrovsk (Dnepropetrovsk—population 1.1 million). This busy river port and railroad junction also has more than 3,300 acres (1,335 hectares) of parks. Mining and metalworking caused the rapid growth of Donetsk (population 1.1 million), an industrial center in southeastern Ukraine.

Ukraine's main seaport is Odesa (Odessa), on the northwestern shore of the Black Sea. People from more than one hundred countries make up Odesa's population of 1 million. Many are ancestors of immigrants who were encouraged to settle in the region by the Russian government in the 1800s. The city's name derives from Odesos, a Greek colony built on the site in the fourth century B.C. A manufacturing

Commuters cross cobble-stone streets in front of **the train station in Lviv.**

and trading center, Odesa is the site of a large shipbuilding industry. One of the first motion picture studios in the Russian Empire was built in Odesa, which still has an active film industry.

Lviv (Lvov), the principal city in western Ukraine, has a population of 798,000. The Ukrainian king Danylo (Daniel) Halytsky, who built the city in the thirteenth century, named it after his son Lev. Narrow cobblestone streets and ancient buildings have survived in the Old Lviv neighborhood, which also boasts many parks and cafés. Ivan Franko University, founded in 1661 and named after a famous Ukrainian writer, is one of the oldest universities in Europe. Lviv's railways and roads link the city to the rest of Europe and help Ukrainian companies ship their goods to foreign markets. Factories in Lviv make machinery, chemicals, heavy vehicles, electrical equipment, and processed food.

For links to additional information about city life in Ukraine, visit www.vgsbooks.com.

# HISTORY AND GOVERNMENT

Historians know little of Ukraine's prehistoric past, but archaeological finds have shown evidence of human activity in Ukraine dating back to 150,000 B.C. The earliest known farmers in Ukraine were the Trypillians (4500–2000 B.C.), who inhabited settlements along the Dnipro River, south of modern-day Kyiv. The Trypillians lived in long, rectangular log houses that sheltered clans of fifteen to twenty people each. They cultivated wheat, barley, millet, and rye and tamed wild horses, sheep, pigs, and cattle.

Beginning in about 1000 B.C., a succession of nomadic peoples migrated to the steppes of Ukraine. First came the Cimmerians, a people whose origins are largely unknown but who probably came from Persia (modern-day Iran). In about the eighth century B.C., the Scythians, a warrior people from central Asia, entered the area. Skilled horse-mounted warriors, the powerful Scythians drove the Cimmerians out during a bloody thirty-year war, creating an empire that eventually spanned from southern Russia to the Middle East. The

region north of the Black Sea would be known as Scythia for more than one thousand years.

Meanwhile, the Greeks established colonies on the shores of the Black Sea, in the Crimean Peninsula, and along the coast of the Sea of Azov. Greek merchants engaged in trade with their inland Scythian neighbors.

Scythian society was aristocratic, ruled by a monarch who was supported by a small group of wealthy nobles. Most common folk raised cattle and lived and moved from place to place in search of grazing land. Virtually all Scythians owned horses, and riding skill was a vital part of the empire's culture. Scythian soldiers were legendary for their brutality. For example, they sawed off the tops of slain enemies' heads to present them as trophies to their commanders in exchange for a share of the spoils of war.

During the fourth century B.C., Scythian dominance was challenged by another nomadic people from central Asia—the Sarmatians. The Sarmatians were also skilled in the use of horses and warfare and practiced a similar lifestyle. Their conquest of the region was complete by about the second century B.C., and its domination lasted until the A.D. 200s, when invaders from northern Europe, the Goths, conquered the area.

Gothic supremacy lasted less than two hundred years. In about 375, the Huns, a warrior people from the east, drove the Goths out of the region. In the following centuries, a succession of nomadic invaders—the Bulgars, Avars, and others—conquered and occupied the steppe. During this period, the Greek settlements in the south declined, while the Slavs, an ethnic group from north of the Carpathian Mountains, settled in the forests of northern and western Ukraine. The Slavs are the direct ancestors of modern Ukrainians. By the sixth century, Slavic groups were settling the land near Kyiv and creating a new state that would grow into a mighty empire.

## Kyivan Rus

History books known as chronicles describe much of Ukraine's past. The most famous of these works, *The Tale of Bygone Years* (ca. 1113), was compiled by a Ukrainian monk named Nestor. It describes the legendary founders of Kyiv—the Slavic prince Kyi and his family, who lived in the seventh century. Located on the western banks of the Dnipro, Kyiv prospered through its control of trade along this increasingly important waterway. The growing city's success attracted the attention of outsiders,

A monument in Kyiv depicts **Prince Kyi and his brothers and sister,** the legendary seventh-century founders of Kyiv described in *The Tale of Bygone Years.*

however, who sought to gain control of the area.

In the middle of the ninth century, Varangian Rus traders from Sweden entered Ukraine. In 882 the Rus prince Oleg, from Novgorod in northwestern Russia, declared himself ruler of Kyiv. Historians disagree over whether the Varangian Rus conquered the region or were invited to establish their rule. Nevertheless, Oleg's family, the Ruriks, set up a dynasty (family of rulers) that would rule Kyiv for many years. Under Rurik power, Kyivan Rus, as the kingdom came to be called, grew and prospered until it became the most powerful state in Europe. The kingdom stretched from the Baltic Sea to the Danube River (in central Europe) to the Volga River in southern Russia. Over time, the Rus rulers came to adopt the Slavic language and Slavic culture of the region.

Volodymyr the Great, who lived during the tenth century, was the fourth member of the Rurik dynasty to rule Kyivan Rus. Seeking a way to unify the Slavic peoples of the region, Volodymyr converted to Christianity in the 980s. He then required all of his subjects to accept the Christian faith. When Christianity split into the Roman Catholic Church and the Eastern Orthodox Church in the eleventh century, Kyivan Rus aligned with the Orthodox branch of the church.

Kyiv, the political center of Kyivan Rus, continued to thrive as a commercial city. It controlled much of the trade between northern Europe and the Byzantine Empire, whose capital—Constantinople—was located to the south in modern-day Turkey. The Greek-speaking Byzantine Empire, the center of the Orthodox faith, also influenced the culture, religion, and language of Kyivan Rus.

Volodymyr's son and successor, Yaroslav the Wise, further developed Kyivan Rus by building schools and churches, by establishing written laws, and by promoting the arts. He forged close ties with other

## THE TALE OF BYGONE YEARS

*The Tale of Bygone Years* describes how the peoples of the area invited the Varangian Rus to rule over their lawless realm (although some modern historians have questioned this version of events):

"There was no law among them, but tribe rose against tribe. Discord thus ensued among them, and they began to make war against one another. They said to themselves, 'Let us seek a prince who may rule over us, and judge us according to the law.' They accordingly went overseas to the Varangian Russes. . . . [They] said to the people of Rus: 'Our land is great and rich, but there is no order in it. Come to rule and reign over us.'"

–Journalist-historian Anna Reid quoting *The Tale of Bygone Years*

nations by marrying his three sons and three daughters into European royal families. But after Yaroslav's death in 1054, the realm broke into separate principalities that were ruled by his many relatives.

## The Galicia-Volhynia Principality

The breakup of Kyivan Rus left the Slavic state with weakened defenses. In the thirteenth century, the Mongol Tatars, ruthless horse-mounted warriors from central Asia, swept across eastern Europe. In 1240 the era of Kyivan Rus came to a close when the Tatars attacked Kyiv, laying waste to the city and forcing most of the region's surviving inhabitants to flee. The Tatars also seized control of the Crimea, which they would rule for the next several centuries.

Meanwhile, refugees from Kyiv and other parts of Ukraine moved westward to escape the Tatars. Many settled in the Galicia-Volhynia principality, which was in what became western Ukraine. This state remained independent until 1340, when the death of the last Galician prince caused a struggle for control of the region among the powers of eastern Europe. Galicia fell to Poland, and the region of Volhynia became part of Lithuania, a powerful state north of Ukraine.

When Lithuania united with Poland in 1569, these lands and the city of Kyiv came under the rule of the Polish king. As subjects of Poland, the Ukrainian people were forced to become serfs—farm laborers who were the property of *szlachta* (landowners). In addition, the Poles introduced the Polish language and attempted to convert Orthodox believers to Roman Catholicism, the faith of the Polish people. In 1596 a compromise was agreed upon between Orthodox and Roman Catholics, and nobles and religious leaders signed an Act of Union. The act created a new Uniate Church, in which worshipers and clergy acknowledged the supremacy of the Roman Catholic pope but were allowed to continue most of their Orthodox customs.

Yet many Ukrainians resisted these changes and sought to achieve freedom from outside rule. Some of them organized brotherhoods,

### THE MONGOL HORDE

The Mongol Tatars who invaded Europe in the thirteenth century were often referred to as the Mongol Horde. Feared for their savagery and fighting skills, one chronicler described them as a "darkness chased by a cloud."

Before invading the city in 1240, Batu Khan, leader of the Mongol Tatars, promised to "tie Kyiv to his horse's tail." During the sack of the city, the invaders killed thousands and burned more than four hundred churches. Thousands more people fled the city.

which undertook educational and religious work. The brotherhoods began in Lviv and spread to other cities. In addition, a new Ukrainian Orthodox leadership was established in Kyiv in 1620. In 1631 the Kyivan metropolitan (church leader) Petro Mohyla founded the Kyiv Mohyla Academy, the first Ukrainian institution of higher learning.

## The Cossacks

During this same period, groups of people were gradually returning to areas of central Ukraine that had been abandoned in the wake of the Tatar invasion. Many of these Slavic speakers came from Poland and from Lithuanian lands to the north and west. Most were former serfs who traveled south in search of freedom and to fish and hunt in the frontier regions of the Ukrainian steppes. In time, they adopted the horse-mounted military tech-niques of the Tatars and organized self-governing com-munities. Known as Kazakhs (Cossacks in English), from a Turkic-language word meaning "outlaw, adven-turer, or free person," they gained enough strength over time to be able to resist the harsh rule of the Polish king.

> "The Cossacks are to the Ukrainian national consciousness what cowboys are to the American. . . . They ranged the steppe in covered wag-ons, drawing them up into squares in case of Tatar attack. . . . They wore splendid moustaches, red boots and baggy trousers 'as wide as the Black Sea.' They danced, sang, and drank *horilka* [vodka] in heroic quantities."
>
> —journalist-historian Anna Reid

The Cossacks were a disciplined group. They elected their own body of lawmakers (*rada*) and hetmans (leaders) in raucous outdoor meetings. With their reputation as the best fighting force in Europe, the Cossacks attracted peasants, nobles, and even some foreigners to their *sichs,* or settlements. The most famous of these settlements, the Zaporozhian Sich, was a fortified town located on an island on the lower Dnipro River. For about two hundred years, the Cossacks remained the strongest defenders of the Ukrainian people and of the Ukrainian Orthodox Church.

Although the kings of Poland had little control of the Cossacks, these rulers needed allies to fight the Tatars and other invaders. The Poles created and financed units of "registered Cossacks," who lived on their own land and who helped the Polish army in time of need. Other Cossacks inhabited fortified settlements and fought for whomever they pleased.

This statue of Bohdan Khmelnytsky, the Ukrainian revolutionary, stands in Kyiv.

## Cossack Uprisings and "Little Russia"

The harsh conditions—serfdom in particular—suffered by Ukrainians under the Polish kings created conditions ripe for violent revolts by peasants and Cossacks. The hetman Bohdan Khmelnytsky led the largest such revolt. A Polish szlachta himself, he was inspired by a personal grudge to flee Poland and join the Cossacks. He soon became the leader of the Zaporozhian Sich, and in the spring of 1648, Khmelnytsky's Cossacks joined forces with four thousand Tatar horse-mounted soldiers. Together this group crushed an invading Polish army in a decisive battle.

The victory inspired a massive uprising against Polish rule and those who supported it. Cossacks and peasants marched toward the Polish capital of Warsaw, leaving destruction in their wake. In a wave of violence, the rebels slaughtered Catholic priests, Polish szlachta, government officials, and Jews. (Jews were unpopular because many worked for landowners or held positions as tax collectors). The Poles responded with equally brutal attacks against Cossacks.

For three years, Khmelnytsky's hetmanate (hetman-led territory) covered all of western and central Ukraine. But in 1651, his Tatar allies deserted him and the Poles defeated him. In need of military aid, Khmelnytsky sought help from the czar (emperor) of Russia, whose empire lay northeast of Ukraine. In 1654, in exchange for Russian aid, Khmelnytsky swore an oath of loyalty to the czar and signed the Treaty of Pereiaslav. This fateful agreement would have a deep and lasting effect on the future of Ukraine.

The two parties had strongly differing views on the meaning of the treaty. While the Cossacks believed the agreement assured them independence, the Russians claimed that the Cossacks had submitted to the czar and began to call the area "Little Russia."

Whatever the case, the treaty failed to bring peace to the region. For the next thirty years, the area was wracked by war as Russian, Polish, Tatar, and Cossack armies fought for control. This period, known as "The Ruin" in Ukrainian history, finally ended in 1686, when Poland and Russia divided the region between themselves. Russia seized lands to the east of the Dnipro, while Poland took over territory to the west. These east-west and Polish-Russian divisions are still seen in modern times in Ukraine's language, culture, and religion.

## The End of the Cossacks and New Russia

The Cossacks were not consulted in the Polish-Russian agreement of 1686—a sign of their waning power and influence. But in the following decades, several Cossack leaders attempted to regain control of Ukraine. In the early 1700s, Hetman Ivan Mazepa joined forces with King Charles XII of Sweden against Russian czar Peter I. But the Russians defeated the Swedes and the Cossacks at the Battle of Poltava in 1709. Peter I then used Cossack prisoners as forced labor to build canals and cities in the Russian Empire.

In 1774 Russian empress Catherine II signed a peace treaty with Russia's long-standing rival, the Ottoman Empire, which, at the time, controlled the Crimean Peninsula. The treaty not only awarded the Russians control of the Crimea but also eliminated a major outside threat. Since the Cossack protection was no longer useful to Russia, the following year, Catherine II sent troops to crush the Cossacks once and for all. By 1781 the hetmanate had ceased to exist. The remaining hetmans became Russian nobles (landowners), and their subjects became serfs. Catherine added Ukrainian territory west of the Dnipro River to her realm. Decades later, Galicia became part of the Austro-Hungarian Empire.

Russian czar Peter I, also known as **Peter the Great,** defeated a Cossack attempt to regain independence from Russia in the early 1700s.

The Russian empress named the area New Russia and placed its capital in Odesa. The Russians then set about making use of its rich farmland. Settlers from Russia, as well as from other parts of Europe—Serbia, Armenia, Moldova, Greece, Germany, Switzerland, and numerous other places—were encouraged to move in. Throughout the nineteenth century, farms, villages, cities, and towns sprang up in southern Ukraine and in the Crimea. Russia benefited from Ukraine's productive agriculture and growing industry, but most Ukrainians lived in poverty with few rights as citizens. Serfdom was eventually abolished in the mid-1800s, but common Ukrainians still had no representation in government and few legal rights.

At the same time, Russia sought to suppress any Ukrainian ideas of separateness or independence from Russia. To do this, they imposed

**Alexander II**

Russian culture and institutions through Russification programs. The Russians forced many Uniate churches to become Orthodox. In 1876 Czar Alexander II attempted to make the Ukrainian language extinct. He signed a decree that banned the publication of Ukrainian books and newspapers, that forbade the production of stage shows and lectures in the Ukrainian language, and that made it illegal to teach the language in schools. All Ukrainian books were banned from libraries.

A movement to keep the Ukrainian language and Ukrainian culture alive lived on among some Ukrainians, especially in Austrian-controlled Galicia. The movement's two most prominent leaders were Professor Mykhailo Hrushevsky, a historian who published an extensive history of Ukraine, and Taras Shevchenko who wrote about the Ukrainian people. But by the end of the nineteenth century, the dream of Ukraine as an independent nation seemed a long way from becoming reality.

## War, Revolution, and Civil War

By the early twentieth century, widespread hunger and poverty were causing increasing discontent within the Russian Empire. Czar Nicholas II was widely seen as a weak ruler with little interest in improving the lives of the empire's citizens.

In 1914 World War I broke out in Europe. This global conflict pitted Russia, France, and Britain (often called the Allies) against the Central Powers, which were led by Germany and Austria-Hungary. Millions of Ukrainians were called on to fight. In eastern Ukraine, the Russians drafted about 3.5 million Ukrainians to fight against the

Central Powers, while the Austrians drafted nearly 250,000 western Ukrainians to fight the Russians. Galicia and other parts of Ukraine soon became a battleground for these forces. As tens of thousands of soldiers on both sides died in pitched battles, millions of civilians were killed or displaced by the fighting.

As the war dragged on, Russian armies suffered defeats at the hands of the Central Powers in Ukraine and in other regions. The devastating toll of the war further weakened the crumbling Russian Empire. Revolutionaries, some of them Communists, called for an end to the czar's rule and for the establishment of a new government. Vladimir Ilych Lenin, a leading Communist, promised bread, land, and peace to the empire's workers and peasants. Under Communism, the government controls virtually all aspects of a country's economy. Banks, businesses, and eventually, even farms, became the property of the state.

As the war effort continued to falter, the czar's government crumbled. In March 1917, revolutionaries overthrew the government, and Nicholas II gave up his throne. In the turmoil that followed, a group of Ukrainian officials established a new governing body, the Central Rada to rule eastern Ukraine. Members of the Central Rada elected the Ukrainian history scholar, Professor Mykhailo Hrushevsky, as president of the council. In western Ukraine, a nationalist movement (a movement to create an independent Ukrainian state) was also gaining momentum at this time.

At first the Central Rada was hopeful of establishing a Ukraine that was semi-independent from Russia. But its members—mostly young men with no experience in politics—soon fell into disarray.

A group of **Cossack fighters with their horses** listen to a soldier demonstrate how to use a gas mask. The Cossacks fought again for Ukrainian independence from Russia in the Russian Civil War during the early 1900s.

After the fall of Czar Nicholas II in 1917, historian and political activist **Mykhailo Hrushevsky** was elected as the first president of independent Ukraine.

Hrushevsky and the new leadership was unable to lead the country in the ongoing war or to provide even basic government services. Then, in November 1917, Lenin's Bolshevik Party seized control of Russia, promising to create the world's first Communist state. Soon after, Lenin, desperate to take Russia out of the war, signed a peace treaty with the Central Powers. The treaty handed over a large swath of Ukraine to the Central Powers, and German troops soon occupied the country. In April 1918, the Germans disbanded the Central Rada.

In the coming years, a series of short-lived governments emerged in both eastern and western Ukraine. But these new leaderships proved as ineffective as the Central Rada. Ukraine began to slide into chaos and anarchy (lawlessness) as the area became a battleground for several competing powers. The Allies were alarmed at the prospect of a Communist state in Russia and sent troops to try to defeat the Bolsheviks. Meanwhile, Russians opposed to Communist rule—known collectively as the Whites—formed armies to defeat Lenin's regime.

The situation worsened as the Central Powers neared defeat in 1918 and the German and Austro-Hungarian empires collapsed. As the Germans pulled out of Ukraine, the Polish, the Czech, and the Hungarian armies marched in, hoping to acquire parts of the country.

Ukraine became the scene of a devastating civil war. The conflict destroyed Ukrainian cities and brought widespread famine and disease. About 1.5 million Ukrainian soldiers and civilians died in the conflict. In the spring of 1921, Lenin's Communists finally defeated their opponents. After Poland signed a treaty with Lenin's government, Ukrainian territory was divided among the Communists, Poland, Romania, and Czechoslovakia. The major Ukrainian cities, including Kyiv, came under the control of the Communist government.

The Ukrainian Soviet Socialist Republic became part of the Union of Soviet Socialist Republics (USSR) in 1922. The Ukrainian and Russian republics signed an economic and military union, and Lenin's government stated that Ukraine was an equal partner with Soviet Russia. Yet Ukraine had little independence, and the government of the USSR took over factories, farms, and local governments.

To gain support in the region, the Soviet government allowed Ukraine to preserve its language and permitted Ukrainian farmers to sell their produce on open markets. Ukrainian literature flourished, and a new generation of teachers sought to educate students about Ukrainian history. But these freedoms also led to a revival of Ukrainian nationalism. Intent on keeping strict control of Ukraine and all other parts of the Soviet Union, the new Soviet leader Joseph Stalin responded by purging the country of "counter-revolutionaries," or people he accused of trying to overturn the Communist revolution.

**Joseph Stalin**

Beginning in the late 1920s, Soviet secret police agents arrested thousands of suspected counterrevolutionaries—mostly university teachers and students and Orthodox Church clergy. Most were sent into exile in the wastelands of Siberia in northern and western Russia to be used as slave labor to build numerous Soviet modernization projects, such as canals and dams. Thousands more were simply executed.

For more information about the history of Communism in Ukraine, visit www.vgsbooks.com.

## ◉ Industrialization, Collectivization, and Famine

At the same time, Stalin was embarking on an ambitious plan to make the rural Soviet Union into a leading industrial power. During the First Five-Year Plan (1928–1933), the Soviet leader ordered the digging of new mines and the building of new factories in Ukraine.

The plan also called for the collectivization of Soviet agriculture to give the government more control over agricultural output. Collectivization abolished privately owned family farms. Instead, farmers would work together in collective farms, or kolkhozy, which would be owned and run by the government. Thus, farmers had to give

**Ukrainian farmworkers gather** for a meeting on a collective farm in the 1930s. The Soviet Union's Communist government seized all privately owned farms and created larger state-run farms in the 1920s and 1930s.

up all their land and animals to the collectives. They became ordinary workers on government-owned estates and were paid with small portions of food produced on the collectives. Although the goal of the collectives was to raise mass food production, these large farms tended to be inefficient, and their production was lower than expected.

Many Soviet farmers bitterly resisted giving up their property, with the greatest resistance coming from Ukrainians. In many cases, Communist Party workers who came to impose collectivization were murdered. The Soviet government responded by sending in troops and secret police agents to punish the farmers. During this period, about 6.5 million Ukrainians were executed or exiled to labor camps in Siberia.

But by the early 1930s, many Ukrainians were continuing to resist collectivization. To crush the farmers once and for all, Stalin ordered the seizure of crops and seed grain. Soviet troops, Communist workers, and secret police agents swept through the countryside, stripping the Soviet Union's rural area of food. As a result, about 5 million Ukrainians starved to death in a massive famine. By the mid-1930s, the vast majority of Ukraine had been collectivized and what remained of the country's population had little strength to resist Soviet rule.

## World War II

In the late 1930s, Adolf Hitler and his Nazi Party came to power in Germany. A sworn enemy of Communism, Hitler ordered a rapid buildup of his country's military. He also called for revenge for Germany's defeat in World War I. Thus another major war in Europe appeared inevitable. Yet both Germany and the Soviet Union needed time to get ready for the conflict. To buy time, Germany and the Soviet Union signed the Molotov-Ribbentrop Pact. This agreement banned conflict between the two countries and allowed the Soviets to prepare for war while giving Hitler the freedom to confront his enemies to the west.

By 1941 Hitler had conquered much of western Europe. In June he turned to the Soviet Union, breaking the treaty by attacking Ukraine and other Soviet territories. The Soviet government enlisted Ukrainians to fight Hitler's invading armies. Many Ukrainians, however, saw the Germans as their liberators from Soviet rule and joined the German forces. Other Ukrainians created an underground army to fight both the Germans and the Soviet Red Army.

In 1945 the war—the most costly in history in terms of human life and property—ended with Germany's defeat. The years of conflict had devastated Ukrainian cities, towns, and farms. About 5.3 million people had died—about one out of every six Ukrainians—and countless more had either been deported to Germany as slave labor or had fled the Soviet Union. Among the dead were about 600,000 Ukrainian Jews who had been slaughtered by German troops as part of Hitler's "Final Solution," a program to destroy the entire European Jewish population.

After the war, the Soviet government added territory to Ukraine. Poland surrendered land that is part of western Ukraine. Crimea was transferred from Russia to Ukraine in 1954.

The years following the war also saw an increase in tensions between the Soviet Union and the United States. This period of mutual distrust came to be known as the Cold War (1945–1991). The two rival nations built up large stockpiles of nuclear weapons in preparation for a nuclear confrontation. Ukrainian scientists and Ukrainian

## FAMINE IN UKRAINE

"On a recent visit to the Northern Caucasus and the Ukraine, I saw something of the battle that is going on between the government and the peasants. On the one side, millions of starving peasants, their bodies often swollen from lack of food; on the other, members of the GPU [Soviet secret police] carrying out the instructions of [the Soviet government]. They had gone over the country like a swarm of locusts and [had] taken away everything edible; they had shot or exiled thousands of peasants, sometimes whole villages; they had reduced some of the most fertile land in the world to a melancholy desert."

—British writer Malcolm Muggeridge, 1933

**Nikita Khrushchev**

industry played a major role in developing Soviet nuclear weapons, and many Soviet nuclear missile launch sites were based in Ukraine.

In the 1950s, a Ukrainian, Nikita Khrushchev, succeeded Stalin as leader of the Soviet Union. Khrushchev served in this post until 1964. Huge mills in Ukraine supplied steel for new construction, and collective farms grew enough grain to support the Soviet Union's expanding population. Ukraine became an essential part of the later five-year economic plans that guided the USSR's economy.

## The Struggle for Democracy

Despite the economic strength of Ukraine, years of mismanagement by the Communist government resulted in a sharp economic decline in the late 1970s and early 1980s. The state-owned factories and farms had proved to be inefficient, and shortages of consumer goods and food were common. Communist leaders, who sought to keep control over the USSR's economy, resisted nearly all economic reforms. They also strictly controlled the media and brutally crushed government critics.

This situation changed after Soviet president Mikhail Gorbachev, who came to power in 1985, introduced the policies of glasnost (openness) and perestroika (restructuring). Gorbachev hoped that these policies would foster reform. Instead, the freedom of expression allowed through glasnost opened the floodgates of resentment against Soviet rule, inspiring many Soviet citizens to criticize their government and call for change. Ukrainians also seized the opportunity to revive their traditions and to replace the Russian language with Ukrainian in their schools.

The April 1986 explosion at the Chornobyl nuclear power plant, followed by the Soviet government's slow reaction to it, only intensified anti-Soviet feelings in Ukraine. In September 1989, Ukrainians created a national democratic group called Rukh (meaning "movement" in Ukrainian).

In open elections held in March 1990, prodemocracy candidates won 25 percent of the seats in the Ukrainian parliament. At the same time, independence movements in other Soviet republics were threatening to break up the USSR. To prevent this development, Gorbachev urged the republics to sign a union treaty. This agreement would have granted some independence to Ukraine but would also have reserved important powers for the central Soviet government.

In August 1991, just before Ukraine and other Soviet republics were to sign the treaty, a group of Communists attempted to overthrow Gorbachev. Although this coup d'état failed, the Communist Party's

In February 1990, Ukrainians in Lviv gathered for a **proindependence rally** in the weeks before a nationwide election. At the same time, many Soviet republics sought to gain independence from the weakening Soviet government, which finally collapsed in December 1991.

authority rapidly declined. Ukraine proclaimed its independence on August 24, 1991. By a public vote held in December 1991, an overwhelming 90 percent of Ukrainians approved this action.

Leonid Kravchuk, a former Communist Party official, became Ukraine's president. Kravchuk also adopted the program of Rukh, which called for an independent, democratic Ukraine. On December 25, 1991, Gorbachev resigned, and the Soviet Union formally dissolved. Several nations, including Poland, the United States, and Russia, then recognized Ukraine as an independent country.

## Post-Soviet Ukraine

At the time of independence, many Ukrainians had high hopes for their country's future. But economic difficulties and a resistance to change have largely stalled programs for significant reform. In 1993 runaway inflation devastated the Ukrainian economy. As the value of the country's currency dropped, unemployment and the poverty rate skyrocketed. Amid this turmoil, a 1994 election brought Leonid Kuchma to the presidency. His administration struggled to fix the country's collapsing economy, however. The situation was stabilized somewhat in 1996 with the introduction of a new currency, the hryvnia. But another serious financial crisis erupted in 1998, leaving many more Ukrainians unemployed and homeless.

Other attempts to reform and improve the country's economy have been largely unsuccessful. International observers believe that the Ukrainian government can improve its situation by privatizing, or sell-

**Election officials watch carefully** as voters place ballots into sealed ballot boxes during the 2004 presidential elections. Charges of voter intimidation, ballot box stuffing, and other irregularities led the Ukrainian Supreme Court to declare the election results invalid.

ing to public bidders, many of its large, inefficient, government-controlled businesses. Yet privatization has occurred only sporadically, and the sales have more often served the interests of a few wealthy businesspeople and politicians, instead of the public as a whole.

Experts also believe that decollectivizing the country's farms and handing them off to private owners would increase their efficiency. But Ukrainian farmers have strongly resisted such changes, mostly out of fear that the farms would end up in the hands of a few wealthy individuals.

In 2003 the Ukrainian government lent its support to the United States by sending 1,600 Ukrainian troops to Iraq after a U.S.-led group of nations invaded the country to remove from power Iraqi president Saddam Hussein. Ukrainian forces helped to rebuild the country as it worked toward electing a new government.

The flawed first round of the 2004 presidential elections and the mass protests that followed placed Ukraine squarely in the world spotlight. These events also highlighted the sometimes bitter divisions between generally pro-Russian eastern Ukraine and the more pro-Western central and western Ukraine. The majority of international election observers judged the final December 26 rerun as fair, although some cases of fraud and abuse were recorded. New president Viktor Yushchenko has pledged to work hard to bring the country together after this tense period.

# Government

The Ukrainian constitution was adopted on June 28, 1996, and allows voting rights for all citizens aged eighteen or older. The government of Ukraine is made up of legislative, executive, and judicial branches. The Ukrainian legislature, known as the Verkhovna Rada (Supreme

Council), debates and passes laws. Its 450 members, known as deputies, are elected to four-year terms. The executive branch is headed by a president, who is elected to a five-year term via direct popular vote. The president signs legislation passed by the Verkhovna Rada and is commander in chief of the armed forces. The president also appoints a cabinet of ministers that oversees various areas of government, such as foreign affairs, agriculture, and commerce. A prime minister heads the cabinet. The Verkhovna Rada elects the five judges to the highest court in Ukraine's judicial system, the Supreme Court of Ukraine. Judges serve five-year terms.

Ukraine is divided into many units for administration. It consists of 24 oblasts (administrative units) and two municipalities, or urban political units (Kyiv and Sevastopol). The Crimean Peninsula, while still part of Ukraine, is an autonomous (self-ruled) republic.

## POISONED?

In the summer of 2004, a few weeks before the first round of the presidential elections, candidate Viktor Yushchenko became gravely ill after having dinner with a Ukrainian secret police official. He was hospitalized for several days with severe abdominal pain, swelling of his internal organs, and ulcers (sores) in his digestive tract. He had gruesome skin lesions on his face and body, which left his skin disfigured.

Despite his illness, Yushchenko returned to campaigning. He accused his opponents of poisoning him, also noting that unknown vehicles had tried to run him off the road on two previous occasions. His main rival, Viktor Yanukovych, denied the charges. Yet medical tests confirmed that Yushchenko's illness had been caused by the ingestion of a high dose of a poison, dioxin. Little is known about treatment and long-term consequences of the poisoning, since no one is known to have survived such a high dose of dioxin before.

**Photos taken of Viktor Yushchenko** in January 2004 *(left)* and in November 2004 *(right)* reveal the disfiguring effects of dioxin poisoning.

# THE PEOPLE

The population of Ukraine is 48.1 million, but this number is declining due to a combination of a low birthrate and a relatively high emigration rate. On average, a Ukrainian woman produces only 1.4 children in her lifetime, and only 10 births take place for every 16 deaths. The Population Reference Bureau projects a continued decline in the number of people living in Ukraine, to 45.1 million by 2025 and 38.3 million by 2050. This phenomenon is also occurring in Ukraine's post-Soviet neighbors of Belarus and Russia. Financial hardship and difficult social conditions are generally regarded as the cause for the declining birthrate.

Political persecution has also driven many Ukrainians to leave their homeland over the decades. In the early 2000s, about 22.5 million Ukrainians live outside of Ukraine, with more than 1.5 million in the United States and 1 million in Canada. The South American nations of Brazil (350,000) and Argentina (220,000) also have large Ukrainian populations, while western European countries such as Great Britain (35,000), France (30,000) and Germany (20,000) are home

to a significant number of Ukrainians. Most of the Ukrainian diaspora (people living far from their homelands) reside in the former Soviet republics or in eastern Europe.

## Ethnic Mixture and Language

Nearly all Ukrainians are ethnic Slavs—ancestors of the Slavic peoples who moved into the area beginning in the fourth century. Within Ukraine itself, Ukrainians are categorized by the language they speak. About 78 percent of the population is ethnic Ukrainian—meaning persons of Slavic background who speak the Ukrainian language. Ethnic Russians make up roughly 17 percent of the population. Most of the country's Russian speakers reside in Ukraine's industrialized east or in the Crimean Peninsula. Other groups living in Ukraine make up the remainder of Ukraine's ethnic mix. They include small numbers of Belarusians, Moldovans, Bulgarians, Hungarians, Romanians, Poles, Crimean Tatars, and Jews.

## THE CRIMEAN TATARS

For hundreds of years, the Crimean Peninsula was home to a large population of Tatars. These descendants of the Mongol Tatars ruled the peninsula for centuries. They swore loyalty to the Ottoman Turks—a Muslim empire based in Turkey.

German troops occupied the Crimea during World War II. After Soviet troops drove the Germans out in 1944, Soviet leader Joseph Stalin accused the Crimean Tatar population of collaborating with the enemy. He ordered the removal of the entire population. Over three days, Soviet secret police units packed up nearly all of the 250,000 Tatars into railroad cars. Without food or water, they were sent eastward to barren locations in central Asia. About half the population died either en route or within the first year in their new settlements. In 1989 Soviet leader Mikhail Gorbachev allowed the Crimean Tatars to move back to their homeland. About 250,000 have returned, but their lands have long since been occupied by Russians. Their future remains uncertain.

Even before independence, in 1991, Ukrainian was made the country's official language (except in the Crimea, where Russian remains the official language). The 1996 constitution calls for Ukrainian to be taught in schools. However, this change has not been strictly enforced, and Russian is still taught in many public schools.

Russian also remains the main language of business in Ukraine—primarily due to the country's strong business ties to Russia. However, Ukrainian is the language of the government, and most public signs and billboards are in Ukrainian. This mix is a reflection of Ukraine's unique mingling of different-yet-similar ethnic groups. Ukrainians living in Lviv speak Ukrainian almost exclusively, distinguishing themselves from the mostly Russian-speaking east. People living in the central part of the country may speak Russian, Ukrainian, or most likely both.

Learning and speaking both languages is not a tremendous challenge, since they are very similar. Both Russian and Ukrainian (as well as Belarusian) use the Cyrillic alphabet, which is based on Greek letters. They also share many of the same or similar words, although they are often pronounced differently. For example, the Ukrainian word for "hi" is pronounced *prihVEET*, while the Russian "hi" is pronounced *preeVYET*.

Ukraine's history as an outlawed language has kept a standard form of Ukrainian from developing. Instead, the language has many regional dialects and freely borrows words from other languages. As one might expect, Ukrainian spoken

**Dr. Anatol Lysyj (left),** a representative of the Metropolitan Council of the Ukrainian Orthodox Church of the USA, receives a Saint Volodymir medal. He is being honored for his charitable contributions by Patriarch Filaret (right), the head of the Ukrainian Orthodox Church in Kyiv. Many Ukrainians who live in other countries maintain strong ties to their homeland.

in western Ukraine contains many Polish words, while dialects spoken in the east have many Russian terms. The language also borrows many technical terms from German and English.

As with many languages, a noticeable difference exists between written and spoken Ukrainian. Ukrainian that is spoken in speeches and read in literature is much more formal than the everyday Ukrainian used in conversation.

Visit www.vgsbooks.com to find a link to the Ukrainian World Congress, an organization that seeks to preserve the identity of Ukrainians living outside the country.

## Education

Centuries ago, under Cossack rule, many Ukrainians enjoyed access to education. The ethnic Ukrainian population was among the best educated in Europe. But the situation changed under Russian rule, as policies of neglect and Russification eroded the education system.

Following the Communist takeover in the late 1910s and the Russian Civil War that immediately followed, education was made a high priority throughout the Soviet Union. Literacy—the ability to read and write—for all citizens was considered a vital element in a successful Communist state. As a result, nearly all Ukrainians are literate.

However, the Soviet education system had its limits. Students learned lessons by rote—by memorizing and repeating facts and figures. The Soviet government also strictly controlled what students

**Fifth graders in a classroom in Lviv.** Education is a high priority among Ukrainians, but lack of government resources has left many schools underfunded. For a link to facts and statistics about Ukraine, visit www.vgsbooks.com.

could read and study, and lessons usually contained pro-Communist and anti-Western propaganda. Thus Ukrainians were discouraged from thinking independently and from practicing problem-solving skills. Since independence, the biggest change to Ukraine's education system has been the switch to Ukrainian as the main teaching language. But the old system of rote teaching is still the norm in most schools.

The roles and behavior of students and teachers in Ukrainian classrooms are quite different than they are in the United States or Canada. Ukrainian teachers and professors expect to be treated as superiors. Interrupting or questioning lecturers is considered rude and disrespectful. At the same time, students often work on exams together to figure out the answers—a method that would be considered cheating in many countries.

Ukrainian children begin school at the age of six. They attend four years of elementary school, followed by seven years of secondary school. Education is compulsory through the ninth grade, called the ninth form. From there, many students take two more years of secondary school in preparation for entering a university or technical college.

About 70 percent of Ukrainians have a secondary or higher education. Secondary schools offer a variety of subjects and guide students in independent work. Some secondary schools emphasize a particular area of study, such as English or computer programming. After graduating from secondary school, students must take a competitive exam to gain admission to an institute or university. More than 700 technical colleges train workers in job skills. Postsecondary schools in Ukraine number more than 100, including 10 universities—all of which are located in urban areas.

One of the most famous universities in Ukraine is Kyiv Mohyla Academy. Originally founded in 1615, it was the first institution of higher education in Ukraine. During the 1700s, the academy was one of the finest schools in the Orthodox Christian world, and many government officials of the Russian Empire were educated there. The school was also a hotbed for the Ukrainian independence movement, and was therefore closed by Czar Alexander I in the early-1800s.

The academy was reopened in 1992 after independence. It has become one of the most prestigious schools in the former Soviet Union, with a student body of more than two thousand. The school's curricula includes courses in history, philosophy, cultural studies, business, political studies, and biology.

## Health

Under Communism, all citizens had a right to free health care, although the quality of equipment and medical staff was often lower than Western standards. After independence and the economic crises that followed, the Ukrainian government has struggled to meet the public's needs. Ukraine has a shortage of medical equipment and modern facilities, especially in rural areas.

In the 1990s, a lack of resources led to a breakdown in Ukraine's immunization program. The result was a return of some diseases that had previously been all but wiped out. This period saw a resurgence of diphtheria, a potentially life-threatening illness that often attacks the respiratory system. Tens of thousands of people became ill throughout the post-Soviet states. Thousands died before the epidemic was brought under control.

Lack of resources has also left Ukraine with a substandard water supply, particularly in urban areas. Sewage treatment plants are not always properly maintained, and many water storage facilities are contaminated with industrial chemicals. The situation has led to outbreaks of cholera—a potentially deadly waterborne disease that afflicts the small intestine—in some areas.

About two-thirds of Ukraine's population live in urban areas such as Kyiv, Kharkiv, Odesa, and Dnipropetrovsk. The industrialized east is the most crowded part of the country. The rest of the population lives on farms or in villages.

However, the greatest potential threat to the long-term health of Ukrainians may be radioactive contamination from the Chornobyl explosion. Incidences of infertility (the inability to bear children), birth defects, cancer, and other illnesses that have been linked to exposure to radiation have all risen dramatically since the Chornobyl incident. Meanwhile, many citizens continue to expose themselves to harmful radiation by living in contaminated areas, by drinking water there, and by consuming foods grown in contaminated soil. In most cases, these people have no other options available to them.

Yet despite these challenges, the country has a relatively low infant mortality rate—9 deaths for every 1,000 live births. This is lower than in neighboring Russia (13 per 1,000 live births) and in Romania (17 per 1,000) but higher than in Belarus (8 per 1,000) and Poland (7 per 1,000). Life expectancy among Ukrainians is 68 years—nearly the same as neighboring Belarus (69 years) but higher than Russia (65 years). However, this figure is significantly lower than life expectancy in the United States (77 years) and Canada (79 years). Medical experts cite a number of factors for Ukraine's relatively low life expectancy—cigarette smoking (most Ukrainians, especially men, smoke), malnutrition, stress, and lack of exercise. Chornobyl's long-term effects on these statistics have yet to be determined.

HIV/AIDS In the 2000s, Ukraine is experiencing one of the largest HIV/AIDS epidemics in eastern Europe. (HIV, or the human immunodeficiency virus, is the virus that causes the deadly disease AIDS, or acquired immunodeficiency syndrome.) More than 500,000 Ukrainians are infected with HIV—about 1 percent of the population—and thousands die from AIDS each year. A recent study showed intravenous drug use (HIV/AIDS can be spread by sharing infected needles) to be the primary cause of this epidemic, with nearly 70 percent of HIV/AIDS cases coming as a result of sharing dirty needles. To slow the spread of the disease, the government is working with international organizations to help educate the public on the dangers of the disease and how to avoid contracting and spreading it. These organizations have also been distributing antiretroviral drugs, which have been proven to be effective in limiting the effects of HIV. Yet due to a lack of financial resources, far fewer of these drugs have been provided than are needed.

# Women

Ukrainian women are famous for their beauty, and a number of them have become world-famous supermodels. The best-known among these is Milla Jovovich, who was born in Kyiv. In addition to modeling, Jovovich

**A woman sells groceries at a store in Kyiv.** Many Ukrainian women hold jobs outside of the home, a practice that started during Communist rule.

is an accomplished actor and has starred in several films, including *Resident Evil* (2002) and *Messenger: The Story of Joan of Arc* (1999).

Many Ukrainian women have fallen prey to the country's thriving female slave trade. Each year, thousands of young Ukrainian women are kidnapped or duped into traveling overseas, where they are forced into a life of prostitution. The government is making efforts to better educate women about these dangers and how to avoid them.

Under Communist rule, women were expected to work outside the home alongside men. Officially, the Soviet government stated that women should be paid the same amount as men for similar work. In reality, women were usually paid far less. Yet in addition to their duties outside the home, Soviet women were also responsible for maintaining the household, shopping for food and other goods, and caring for the children. The result is that many Ukrainian women feel overworked. In addition, women have borne the brunt of the post-independence era's economic problems. Studies have shown that women are much more likely to be laid off from their jobs than men and that women's wages have dropped in relation to men's since independence.

# CULTURAL LIFE

Under Russian and Soviet rule, Ukrainian culture was often repressed. Since independence, Ukrainians have made an effort to revive their unique traditions. While most Ukrainians share a similar Slavic background, differences in culture can be found in different regions of the country. For example, the Polish-influenced west is home to a large population of Uniates and Catholics, while the Orthodox faith is supreme in the formerly Russian-dominated east.

## Religion

Communist doctrine in the Soviet Union was strictly atheist and deeply hostile to religion. The Soviet Union's Communist rulers strongly discouraged the practice of religion, and at times church leaders and followers suffered persecution under Soviet rule. Authorities destroyed hundreds of Ukrainian churches during the early decades of Communist rule. As a result, many worshipers practiced their faith in private to avoid government harassment.

Religion began to experience a rebirth during the glasnost period of the 1980s. More and more Soviet citizens began to worship openly, while others returned to the faiths that they had abandoned decades earlier. This renaissance of religion reached a high point in 1988, when millions of Ukrainians celebrated the one thousandth anniversary of Kyivan Rus ruler Volodymyr the Great's baptism. In the years following independence, religion has continued to make a comeback, and hundreds of churches, synagogues (Jewish houses of worship), and mosques (Muslim houses of worship) have been built, reopened, or rebuilt. However, many Ukrainians consider themselves nonreligious.

Among Ukrainians who do practice religion, a large majority follow the Eastern Orthodox faith. This branch of Christianity has its roots in Greece and the Byzantine Empire, which was based in modern-day Turkey. Unlike the Roman Catholic Church, which has a single leader in the pope, the Orthodox Church is made up of groups of parishes led by a church leader known as a patriarch.

**Saint Sofia Cathedral** was built in the eleventh century to honor Yaroslav the Wise. The interior contains beautiful frescos (paintings on wet plaster), mosaic floors, and marble decorations.

Within Ukraine itself, the Orthodox Church is further divided between parishes that fall under the control of the patriarch in Kyiv and the patriarch in Moscow, Russia. When Ukraine fell under Russian domination in the seventeenth century, the Ukrainian Orthodox Church was forced to become part of the Russian church. Under Soviet rule, the only official church in Ukraine was the Russian Orthodox Church. Many Ukrainians hope to eventually unite all Orthodox believers under a single patriarch.

The Uniate Church, sometimes known as the Ukrainian Catholic Church, makes up the country's second-largest denomination. The majority of the church's followers live in the western part of the country. The Uniate Church was formed under Polish rule in the late 1500s as a compromise between Polish Catholic and Ukrainian Orthodox worshipers. The Uniate Church follows most Orthodox rites, rituals, and ceremonies but recognizes the Roman Catholic pope as its spiritual leader. The Soviets disbanded the church in 1946, a move that forced its believers to worship in secret. After operating underground for more than four decades, Uniates gained official recognition in the late 1980s and were an important part of the Ukrainian independence movement.

In addition to the Uniate Church, a number of Roman Catholic parishes also exist in Ukraine. Virtually all of these parishes are located in the west, and most serve ethnic Poles and Hungarians. In the years since independence, a number of Protestant Christian groups have gained a foothold in Ukraine. These churches are often staffed by missionaries who have traveled from foreign countries such as the United States to spread their own brand of Christianity to Ukrainian residents.

**Jewish men in Kyiv** gather for a meal at a local synagogue. Ukraine's Jewish population has struggled to survive a long history of persecution.

Ukraine was once home to a large and thriving Jewish population. Kyiv, in particular, at one time had one of the largest Jewish communities in Europe. Yet throughout Ukraine's history, Jews have suffered prejudice and persecution. Hundreds of thousands were massacred during the Cossack uprisings of the 1600s, and the Jewish population was expelled from Kyiv in the early 1800s (they were later allowed to return). Pogroms (organized massacres) erupted in 1881 and 1905, during which citizens slaughtered thousands of Jews. Jews also suffered persecution from all sides during the Russian Civil War, and in the 1930s, the Soviet government closed virtually all synagogues and outlawed the practice of the faith.

The plight of Ukraine's Jews did not end there, however. Under the German occupation during World War II, German officials systematically slaughtered about 600,000 Ukrainian Jews as part of Hitler's "Final Solution." In recent decades, many of Ukraine's Jews have emigrated from Ukraine to the Jewish homeland of Israel. But the small number who remain have sponsored a revival of their faith in Ukraine by opening several synagogues across the country.

Ukraine is also home to a small Muslim population. Most Ukrainian Muslims inhabit Crimea, where the Islamic Ottoman Empire ruled from the 1400s until the late 1800s.

## Food

Ukrainians enjoy a wide variety of tasty foods. Recipes are generally simple and use basic ingredients but are spiced and seasoned to make

**Golubtsy, or stuffed cabbage rolls,** is a traditional Ukrainian food made from ground meat and rice wrapped in cabbage leaves.

them uniquely flavorful. Staple vegetables include beets, cabbages, cucumbers, potatoes, tomatoes, onions, and beans. Ukrainian cooks often use a combination of dill, garlic, and vinegar to add flavor.

Ukraine is often called the "breadbasket of Europe" for good reason. Bread (*khlib* in Ukrainian) is an important part of the Ukrainian diet, and each region of the country boasts its own unique kind. The food's traditional importance is displayed in the tradition of Ukrainians greeting an honored guest by presenting the person with a loaf of bread.

The country's national dish is borshch (borscht). A beet and vegetable soup that originated in Ukraine, borshch is also popular in other Slavic countries (especially Russia). Recipes vary widely by region—some are thick like stew, others thin like soup, some include meat, and others do not. Borshch is always served as an appetizer before a full meal.

*Varenyky,* dumplings filled with meat, potatoes, cheese, or sauerkraut, is another important Ukrainian food. Varenyky is often served on special occasions. *Salo,* raw pig fat that is sometimes flavored with herbs or bacon, is a Ukrainian delicacy. It is usually served on bread. A Ukrainian dish that might be familiar to Americans and Canadians is chicken Kyiv—a boneless, breaded chicken breast stuffed with herbed butter.

Ukrainians also enjoy a wide variety of drinks, from coffee and tea to soft drinks such as Coca-Cola and Pepsi. Alcohol is also consumed widely in Ukraine, with the traditional Slavic drink of vodka the most popular. A lemonadelike drink called kvass, a fermented brew commonly made from rye bread, is also widely consumed.

# BORSHCH

Borshch, the national dish of Ukraine, makes an excellent first course for many meals. This typical recipe includes meat, but many other borshch recipes do not.

1½ pounds beef soup meat with bone

10 to 12 cups cold water

1 teaspoon salt

1 medium onion, chopped

2 medium beets, peeled and cut in thin strips

1 medium carrot, peeled and cut in thin strips

1 medium potato, peeled and diced

½ cup thinly sliced celery

½ cup diced string beans

2 to 3 cups shredded cabbage

¾ cup strained tomatoes or tomato juice

½ clove garlic, peeled and crushed, if desired

1 tablespoon flour

lemon juice

salt and pepper

chopped fresh dill to taste

½ cup sour cream

1. In a large kettle, cover the meat with the cold water. Add the salt and bring slowly to the boiling point. Skim off any excess fat that rises to the top of the water.
2. Cover and simmer for 1½ hours.
3. Add the onion and beets. Cook 10 to 15 minutes, or until the beets are almost done.
4. Add the carrot, potato, celery, and string beans. Continue cooking for about 10 minutes.
5. Put in the cabbage and cook until it is tender. Do not overcook.
6. Stir in the tomatoes or tomato juice and the crushed garlic.
7. Blend the flour with 3 tablespoons of cold water. Spoon into it some soup liquid. Then stir into the borshch. If a thickened borshch is not desired, omit the flour.
8. Add a small quantity of lemon juice, taking care not to use too much. Season to taste with salt and pepper. Bring it to the boiling point. Flavor it with the chopped dill.
9. Just before serving, add a dollop of sour cream.

Serves 6 to 8

A family dressed in traditional Ukrainian clothing stands for a prayer before sitting down to enjoy their **Christmas meal.** Beautiful red borshch is the first course.

## ◎ Holidays and Festivals

Ukrainians observe many Christian holidays, including Christmas and Easter. Church holidays are normally celebrated according to the ancient Roman Julian calendar, which is thirteen days behind the more commonly used Gregorian calendar. As a result, Ukraine's Christmas Day falls on January 7 rather than on December 25.

For Ukraine's Christians, Christmas is the most important holiday of the year. On Christmas Eve, families gather to enjoy a special meal, called Sviata Vecheria (Holy Supper). The supper has twelve courses—one for each of Jesus' apostles. Worshipers then attend church services, sing carols, and pass out gifts to children.

Ukrainian Easter celebrations are also steeped in Orthodox tradition. Worshipers prepare for the holiday throughout the forty-day period of Lent by not eating meat or dairy products and by cleaning and purifying their homes. In the days leading up to Easter, Ukrainian Christians prepare food for the Easter feast. On Easter Sunday, families bring their food to their church to have it blessed by the priest.

Among nonreligious holidays, Independence Day, which falls on August 24, draws the biggest celebrations. Citizens celebrate their country's independence from Soviet rule with fireworks, parades, concerts, festivals, and feasts. March 8 is International Women's Day, during which Ukrainian men and boys celebrate their mothers, wives, and sisters. May 1 is Labor Day, a day for celebrating the country's workers. May 9 is Victory Day, during which Ukrainians celebrate the

Soviet Union's triumph over Germany in World War II. Ukrainians also observe Constitution Day on June 28, the anniversary of the 1996 adoption of independent Ukraine's new constitution.

## ◔ Literature, the Arts, and the Media

As a result of Russification, Ukraine's literary and artistic legacy is rather brief. Nevertheless, a handful of leading figures have achieved the status of national heroes, with the greatest among them poet and artist Taras Shevchenko. During the early 1800s, Shevchenko gained fame by writing about the Ukrainian national identity and the Russian oppression of the Ukrainian people. Shevchenko wrote in Ukrainian, and his brilliant works did much to promote the language of his people. All Ukrainian schoolchildren still read his most famous works, which include *Kobzar, Haidamaky,* and *Hamaliia.*

Historian Mykhailo Hrushevsky is another renowned Ukrainian author. His ten-volume *History of Ukraine-Rus,* published over a period of several decades beginning in 1898, helped to establish Ukraine's identity as an individual nation. He later went on to serve as president of Ukraine for a brief period after the fall of Czar Nicholas II in 1917.

Another writer who promoted the Ukrainian language was Ivan Franko, who lived and wrote in the late 1800s and early 1900s. In addition to writing in a wide variety of media and genres, from fiction and plays to philosophical essays, the multitalented and prolific Franko also translated many European literary masterpieces into the Ukrainian language. Some of his best-known works are *The Turnip Farmer, The Converted Sinner,* and *During Work.* Larysa Kosach, known by her pen name Lesia Ukrainka, wrote powerful poetry in the twentieth century and is considered the country's greatest female poet. One of her finest works, *The Forest Song,* inspired a ballet, an opera, and a motion picture. Isaac Babel wrote vivid short stories of his experiences as a Jew growing up in Odesa and as a soldier in the Russian army during World War I. He later went on to become one of the leading writers of the early Soviet days.

During the Soviet era, strict censorship discouraged most writers from expressing themselves freely. However, a group of Ukrainian poets and prose writers did earn recognition during this time. Perhaps best known among them is Ihor Kalynets, who first began publishing his poetry in the late 1950s. The Soviet authorities considered his works—which were at times critical of the Soviet state—dangerous and imprisoned him in the 1970s.

Under glasnost, Ukrainian writers were finally given the freedom to express their views. Many of the country's finest writers became spokespersons for Ukrainian independence, and their works helped the independence movement gather momentum. Among postindependence writers, Ihor Kalynets remains a leading light. He has written eloquently about his country's postindependence struggles.

Like its writers, Ukraine's visual artists have often struggled to express themselves under foreign rule. But a handful of painters have earned fame, including Taras Shevchenko, who produced more than one thousand pieces of artwork, most of which depicted country life. The most famous of all Ukrainian paintings is Ilya Repin's *Zaporizky Cossacks Writing a Letter to the Turkish Sultan* (1891), a work that captured the rebellious spirit of the Cossacks.

Cossack legends were the source of some of Ukraine's earliest theater productions. But drama, like all of the other Ukrainian arts, was often stifled by foreign rulers. Since independence, many new theaters have opened, and the country boasts more than sixty of them.

Independence has also seen a revival of Ukraine's film industry, and Kyiv hosts an international film festival each year. Ukrainian cinema dates back to the late 1800s, and the country's first film studios were opened in Kyiv and Odesa in 1915. Although few Ukrainian films have earned worldwide acclaim, the best known of them is Ukrainian exile Slavko Novytsky's *The Harvest of Despair* (1972), a documentary that told the story of the Soviet-enforced famine of the early 1930s.

The Soviet government strictly controlled the news media. Before glasnost, newspaper stories and newscasts, for the most part, ignored the country's problems and painted a rosy picture of life in the Soviet Union. Difficulties that were acknowledged by the press were usually blamed on the United States and Europe. After independence, a wave of independent newspapers appeared in Ukraine, each with its own unique voice.

However, the Ukrainian government has still retained control over the country's television news services, and television news coverage rarely criticizes the government. During the 2004 presidential campaign, international observers noted that the opposition candidate, Viktor Yushchenko, received almost no television coverage, while his opponent, Viktor Yanukovych, was shown on the campaign trail daily. The postelection street protests proved to be a landmark moment in the history of the Ukrainian media, when many news organizations defied government orders by broadcasting the protests and questioning the government's handling of the election results.

## Folk Arts and Music

Folk arts are a cherished tradition in Ukraine, and Ukrainian embroidery, weaving, pottery, wood carving, and *pysanky* (decorated Easter eggs) are prized throughout the world. Embroidery is the most popular folk art, and virtually every Ukrainian family can boast of at least one expert in this craft. Embroidered designs are commonly added to shirts, blouses, skirts, towels, and aprons. Intricate and colorful patterns are also a distinctive part of traditional Ukrainian dress. Colors and designs vary throughout the country's different regions, and each village takes pride in having its own unique design.

Weaving, especially of rugs, is another popular Ukrainian craft. Many Ukrainians adorn the walls of their homes with specially woven rugs, known as *kylym.* The intricate geometrical designs of these rugs add beauty to the home, while their heavy fabric provides additional insulation during the cold winter months.

Ukraine's large deposits of kaolin, a clay used for making china, have made the country one of the leading producers of fine pottery. Many Ukrainians make their living by handcrafting colorful vases, bowls, plates, and many other dishes. Wood carving is another important Ukrainian folk craft. Many homes feature elaborately carved woodwork.

By far the most famous kind of Ukrainian folk art is pysanky. Artists create their unique designs by painting wax on hollowed-out eggs and dipping them in dye. When the egg dries, more design is added to it and the egg is dipped in a different color of dye.

Traditional Ukrainian music has Cossack roots. During previous centuries, blind minstrels known as *kobzars* played a stringed instrument known as the *bandura,* while reciting long poems describing Ukrainian history. The bandura has become Ukraine's national instrument, and it can be seen and heard in traditional festivals throughout the country.

**Pysanky are ornately decorated Easter eggs.** Each egg contains symbols and patterns that symbolize Easter. For links to more information on this uniquely Ukrainian artform, visit www.vgsbooks.com.

Ukrainian dancers perform a **traditional folk dance** for an audience in Kyiv. The male dancer in red is doing the hopak.

Traditional music provides the melody and rhythm for the most famous of all Ukrainian folk dances, the *hopak*. This physically demanding dance requires performers to squat down low, kick their legs out, and then jump into the air. The movements were once exercises used by Cossacks to prepare for battle.

Ukrainians also enjoy classical and popular music. One of Ukraine's best-known classical composers is Mykola Lysenko, who wrote operas and symphonies in the late 1800s and often added Ukrainian folk themes to his work.

## Sports and Recreation

Most Ukrainians enjoy spectator sports, with soccer the most popular game. Dynamo Kyiv, the country's best and best-known team, has won several Soviet and European championships over the past several decades. Ukraine has sixteen other professional soccer teams, based in all of the country's major cities. In addition, many Ukrainian soccer players have earned fame and fortune playing for teams throughout Europe.

Ukraine has a long tradition of producing world-class athletes. During the Soviet era, Ukrainians competed in the Olympics and other international competitions under the Soviet Union's banner, usually with great success. Since independence, numerous Ukrainian athletes have brought fame and honor to their homeland by dominating international competition. Among them are figure skater Oksana Baiul, who won independent Ukraine's first gold medal at the 1994 Winter Olympic Games. Swimmer Yana Klotchkova is

**Oksana Baiul after winning an Olympic gold medal in 1994**

**Ukrainian goalkeeper Oleksandr Shovkovsky deflects an attempt on net** in a soccer match against France. Ukraine is in yellow. Ukrainians enjoy watching and playing soccer.

perhaps Ukraine's most popular female athlete. She won two gold medals in both the 2000 and 2004 Summer Olympic Games and is widely regarded as the world's top female swimmer. Gymnast Lilia Podkopayeva earned international fame when she won two gold medals at the 1996 Summer Olympic Games.

Ukrainian athletes have also made their mark in other sports. The Klitschko brothers, Vitali and Wladimir, have both achieved fame for their prowess in the boxing ring. Older brother Vitali earned the title of World Boxing Council heavyweight champion in the mid-2000s. A number of Ukrainians have gone on to enjoy successful careers in the National Hockey League, including Ottawa Senators forward Peter Bondra and Buffalo Sabres defenseman Alexei Zhitnik.

In addition to spectator sports, many Ukrainians enjoy taking part in sporting activities. Soccer and hockey are two of the most popular organized sports, and Ukraine has many youth leagues throughout the country. Ukrainians also enjoy tennis, hiking, bicycling, and many other leisure activities.

To learn more about famous Ukrainian athletes Oksana Baiul and the Klitschko brothers, visit www.vgsbooks.com to find links to their official websites.

# THE ECONOMY

With a highly educated population, a wealth of natural resources, and some of the world's most fertile agricultural land, Ukraine has all the basic elements to become a prosperous nation. Yet before independence, Ukraine's resources were exploited for the benefit of outside powers—first, the Russian Empire, then the Soviet Union. During Soviet times, Ukraine was the "breadbasket" of the Soviet Union, providing the bulk of the country's grain and other agricultural products. Ukraine also served as the heartland for Soviet industry, supplying both raw materials such as coal and iron, as well as factory labor. In addition, the central government in Russia transferred approximately one-fifth of the Ukraine's wealth to fund economic development projects for other Soviet republics, particularly Russia and Kazakhstan.

Following independence, many international economists believed that Ukraine had a chance to thrive once it was freed from its obligations to support the Soviet state—provided the country instituted a wide range of economic reforms. Instead, in the decade following

independence, reform stalled, and Ukraine suffered a devastating economic downturn. Runaway inflation crippled the country's finances and left many citizens impoverished. For example, in the two years between June 1998 and June 2000 alone, the hryvnia, the national currency, lost more than 60 percent of its value. As businesses faltered, millions were left unemployed and homeless. The situation also frightened away potential international investors, denying the country much-needed investment funds. Recent statistics show that about one-third of Ukrainians were living in poverty in the early 2000s.

Ukraine's economic challenges stem from decades of Communist rule, during which government officials in Russia tightly managed the economy. This inefficient and costly system of central management supported a privileged few and caused great hardship for most of Ukraine' s people. The central government controlled the production and distribution of virtually all products. For the most part, military equipment was the highest priority, with a huge portion of the Soviet

In some rural areas of Ukraine, villagers still travel by horse and cart. Ukraine's economy has struggled to adjust to life after Communism.

budget going toward national defense. Consumer goods such as cars and televisions were scarce under Communism and usually available only to privileged party members.

This system needed drastic reforms after independence. But Ukrainian government officials struggled to cope with the changeover from a centrally planned economy to a free-market economy that produced goods and provided services based on supply and demand. In addition, the majority of postindependence government officials were former Communist Party members who had little knowledge or understanding of free-market economics. As economic chaos reigned, further reform stalled. Ukraine's economy began to stabilize in 2001, partially due to reforms implemented by then-prime minister Viktor Yushchenko. The country has enjoyed several years of economic progress since, but the economy still struggles to meet the needs of the population.

Yet some Ukrainians long for a return to the days of Communism and have expressed a willingness to sacrifice their political freedom for more economic stability. However, the majority of Ukrainians continue to have faith in the country's future as a democratic, free-market nation. Many Ukrainians are placing their hopes for future prosperity on new president Viktor Yushchenko's reputation as a reform-minded politician.

Recent statistics show Ukraine's gross domestic product (GDP, the total value of goods and services produced by a country in a year) to be $256.5 billion. This figure is less than one-fourth of the GDP of Russia ($1.282 trillion) but more than four times larger than neighboring Belarus ($62.56 billion). (By further comparison, the GDP of the United States is $10.99 trillion.) Ukraine's economy is fairly evenly divided by sector, with industry making up the largest share of the economy, services falling second, and agriculture last.

# Industry, Mining, and Energy

Industry accounts for almost 42 percent of the Ukrainian GDP and employs 32 percent of the workforce. The heartland of the country's industry lies in the east, in an area that runs along the Donets River basin, or Donbas.

Ukraine's main industries are coal mining, iron mining, steel production, and the manufacture of heavy machinery, diesel locomotives, and aircraft. Ukraine's rich mineral deposits have made mining an important economic activity. The Donbas is a major center for the mining of coal and iron ore. Ukraine also has the world's largest deposits of manganese ore, a vital component of steel and cast iron. Ukrainian titanium is used in the aircraft and shipbuilding industries.

Ukrainian mines produce graphite and many varieties of clay that can be used for pottery, metal casting, soap, textiles, and bricks. Kaolin is used not only in ceramics but also in medicine and in aluminum. Ukraine also has significant deposits of marble, gold, gemstones, and semiprecious stones. An almost inexhaustible supply of salt exists in several regions, with some layers more than 600 feet (183 m) thick.

Due to neglect under Communism, Ukraine is home to some of the most dangerous coal mines in the world. As many as one thousand Ukrainian coal miners have been killed in accidents—such as collapsed tunnels or gas explosions—over the past decade.

**This factory in eastern Ukraine produces steel.**

## CONVERTING TO A PEACETIME INDUSTRY

During the Cold War, Ukraine was home to much of the Soviet Union's defense industry. Ukrainian factories produced tanks, military aircraft, nuclear warheads, missiles, and other weapons. Ukrainian shipyards built warships for the Soviet navy.

Following the breakup of the Soviet Union, many of Ukraine's defense industries have converted to the production of other products. For example, factories that once produced tanks have changed over to making trucks and farm tractors.

The country also has a large chemical industry that produces fertilizer, coke (a byproduct of coal processing that is used for fuel), and sulfuric acid. Ukraine's food-processing industry makes sugar (from sugar beets), flour, pasta, baked goods, meats, vegetables, and dairy products. Oil and margarine are also produced from sunflower seeds.

Ukraine relies mostly on oil and natural gas to supply its energy needs. Fossil fuels produce nearly half of the country's energy. Although the country has significant reserves of these resources, they have yet to be tapped fully. As a result, Ukraine imports most of its oil and natural gas from other countries, particularly Russia.

Nuclear power is the country's second-most important energy source, providing about 43 percent the country's electricity. Ukraine does have its own supplies of uranium, an element needed in the production of nuclear energy. But many Ukrainians have called for a halt to nuclear power use in the wake of the Chornobyl accident. Hydroelectric power provides most of the remainder of Ukraine's energy needs (about 8 percent). Most of the country's hydroelectric plants are part of a huge system of dams and reservoirs that lies along the Dnipro River.

## Services, Tourism, and Trade

The service sector makes up the second-largest portion of Ukraine's economy, accounting for 35 percent of the GDP and employing 44 percent of the workforce. The country's major service industries include government, education, health care, banking, scientific research, engineering, transportation, and trade.

Due to the Soviet government's strict travel restrictions, few outsiders were allowed to visit the Soviet Union. But the resorts along the Black Sea coast were among the most popular destinations for Soviet tourists. Since independence, Ukraine's tourist industry has experienced strong growth, as more and more travelers from foreign countries have arrived to explore Ukraine's rich history and culture. While the Crimea remains the country's prime tourist spot, travelers are also

Thousands of **tourists visit the beaches of the Black Sea** each year. Tourism is a major source of income for the Crimea. Visit www.vgsbooks.com for more information about tourism in the Crimea.

visiting other locations in increasing numbers. Orthodox Christians from around the world travel to Kyiv to learn more about the city's historic ties to their faith and to visit the famous Saint Sofia Cathedral. The natural beauty of the Carpathian Mountains make them a popular destination for hikers, campers, and skiers.

In the 2000s, Ukraine is experiencing a trade surplus, meaning it exports more products than it imports. Ukraine's chief export products are iron, steel, petroleum products, chemicals, heavy machinery such as farm equipment, and food products. The country's main imports are oil, natural gas, machinery, and chemicals. Russia is Ukraine's top trading partner, followed by Turkey, Turkmenistan, Germany, and Italy.

## Agriculture

With its relatively flat, rolling plains and rich, black chornozem (soil), Ukraine has long been one of the world's leading agricultural nations. About 57 percent of the land is suitable for farming or pasture, and agriculture makes up roughly 23 percent of the GDP while employing 24 percent of the workforce.

Before independence, Ukraine was the most productive agricultural area in the Soviet Union, supplying much of the nation's food. However, the collectivized farm system—which still exists in independent Ukraine—is highly inefficient. Collective farmworkers receive very low wages and have little incentive to increase production. Instead, many collective farmworkers spend their spare time cultivating small plots of their own land to provide themselves with food and perhaps extra produce to sell for cash. Only about 2 percent of the

**Sugar beets** are washed and soaked before they are processed into refined sugar. Ukraine's mild climate and rich soil produces the most sugar beets in the world.

A lack of modern equipment is common on Ukraine's farms. Tractors are scarce and are often very old and in disrepair. Many farms still use horses and wagons because tractors and tractor fuel are unaffordable.

country's farms are privately owned, and these are the most productive in Ukraine.

Since independence, the Ukrainian government has discussed redistributing land to private farmers, but these ideas have met resistance from farmers who fear that privatization may increase their hardship. Farmers fear the instability of private ownership, as opposed to the reliability of small but regular salaries. They also have expressed concern that farms could wind up in the hands of wealthy investors instead of the farmers themselves.

Yet despite these challenges, Ukraine's agricultural sector remains a vital part of the country's economy and identity. Wheat and sugar beets are the two biggest crops. In fact, Ukraine is the world's largest producer of sugar beets. Farmers also raise barley, corn, oats, rye, millet, and buckwheat. Other food crops include potatoes, vegetables, melons, berries, grapes, and nuts. Sunflower seeds are produced in large numbers, mostly for use in oil and margarine. Tobacco and wine grapes grow in the hills of southwestern Ukraine and on the Crimean Peninsula. Livestock raised in Ukraine include cattle, sheep, poultry, and pigs.

Visit www.vgsbooks.com for links to websites with additional information about Ukraine's economy.

# Transportation and Communications

Ukraine's transportation network has a total of 105,317 miles (169,491 km) of highways, most of which are paved. Major roadways link all major cities within Ukraine and also connect to major cities within the former Soviet republics. Railways also connect Ukraine's cities. Most of the country's 13,964 miles (22,473 km) of track are set in the Donbas region and are used to transport raw materials such as coal.

In the 1960s and 1970s, Soviet leaders built an extensive pipeline network across Ukraine to transport Soviet oil and natural gas to Europe. The network is still in use in the 2000s and is the main means of transport for Russian oil and gas. The Ukrainian government also uses these pipelines to transport Ukrainian oil and natural gas from one part of Ukraine to another. Ukraine's pipeline system is a major asset for the country, as it gives the Ukrainian government a position of strength in negotiations with Russia.

Russia also relies on Ukraine as a home for the Russian navy's Black Sea Fleet, which is based in the Crimean port of Sevastopol. An agreement signed in 1997 allows Russia to lease the port through 2017. Ukraine's other major shipping centers include the Black Sea ports of Odesa, Kherson, Mykolayiv, as well as Mariupol, which is located on the Sea of Azov.

Ukraine's two major national airlines, Air Ukraine and Ukraine International Airlines, provide service to and from Kyiv to countries throughout the world. A third major airline, Dniproavia, handles international flights to and from Dnipropetrovsk, while numerous regional carriers provide domestic service to all large cities.

**A Ukraine International Airlines Boeing 737** prepares for a landing. The airline was founded in 1992.

More than 1 million Ukrainians have access to the Internet, and this number is growing fast. The country has more than 250 local Internet service providers, and Ukrainians in Kyiv and Odesa can even subscribe to the popular U.S. service, America Online (AOL).

The main challenge to Internet expansion is the poor quality of Ukrainian phone lines. Lack of resources has kept the Ukrainian government from updating its telephone system. The country has nearly 11 million lines in use, but recent statistics show that more than 3.5 million applications for telephones could not be satisfied. As a result, an increasing number of Ukrainians are subscribing to mobile phone services. More than 4 million Ukrainians use mobile phones in the early 2000s.

Far more Ukrainians own radios than televisions. There are about 45 million radios in the country. During the Soviet era, televisions were a rare luxury item, usually only available to privileged party members. Since independence, Ukrainian industry has responded to the public's demand for televisions by increasing production. More than 18 million exist in the country.

## ◉ The Future

In 2005 Ukraine faces a crucial moment in its history. After years of despair following independence, the events of the 2004 presidential campaign have energized millions of Ukrainians and have brought hope for the country's future.

But many challenges lie ahead. Drastic reforms of the country's economy are still needed. President Yushchenko has expressed a desire to bring about these changes but will need to earn the support of mem-

**A young Kyivan, dressed in the orange of Viktor Yushchenko's party,** celebrates at a rally in December 2004. The events of late 2004 have energized Ukrainians and have provided the country with optimism as it faces an uncertain future.

bers of the legislature—many of whom are former Communists who are reluctant to work for change. Yushchenko also faces the challenge of uniting a nation fractured by the events of the election. In the weeks leading up to the rerun election, supporters of the losing candidate, Viktor Yanukovych, reopened centuries-old divisions when they hinted that they might call for separation from Ukraine and unification with Russia. Yushchenko must work hard to bring the country together to reach common goals.

At this vital turning point, Ukraine's future is difficult to predict. But with all of the basic elements needed for prosperity, the country has the potential for a bright future.

**CA. 4500–2000 B.C.** An ancient people, later named the Trypillians, inhabit settlements along the Dnipro River, south of modern-day Kyiv.

**CA. 800S B.C.** Scythians from central Asia enter the area, eventually creating an empire that spans from southern Russia to the Middle East.

**CA. 400S B.C.** Sarmatians from central Asia enter the area to challenge Scythian rule.

**CA. A.D. 200** Goths from northern Europe begin to seize control of the region.

**CA. 375** The Huns, a warrior people from Asia, arrive to challenge the Goths.

**882** Oleg of Novgorod (in northwestern Russia) declares himself ruler of Kyiv and establishes the Rurik dynasty. The dynasty's kingdom would come to be known as Kyivan Rus.

**CA. 980** Rurik monarch Volodymyr the Great converts to Orthodox Christianity and imposes his new religion on the population of Kyivan Rus.

**1054** The death of Rurik ruler Yaroslav the Wise begins the breakup of Kyivan Rus.

**1240** Mongol Tatar invaders lay waste to Kyiv, completing the downfall of Kyivan Rus.

**1569** The kingdoms of Lithuania and Poland unite under the Polish king, bringing much of modern-day Ukraine under Polish rule.

**1596** A compromise between Orthodox Christians and Roman Catholics leads to the creation of a new Uniate Church that follows many Orthodox rites of worship while pledging allegiance to the Roman Catholic pope.

**1648** Cossack hetman Bohdan Khmelnytsky leads a massive uprising against Polish rule.

**1654** Khmelnytsky signs the Treaty of Pereiaslav with the Russian government, setting in motion a long period of Russian rule.

**1774** Russian czarina Catherine II signs an agreement with the Ottoman Empire that grants Russian control of the Crimean Peninsula.

**1840** Ukrainian poet Taras Shevchenko publishes his first collection of poetry, *Kobzar*.

**1876** Czar Alexander II bans the publication of all Ukrainian language books and newspapers.

**1898** Professor Mykhailo Hrushevsky publishes the first volume of his ten-volume *History of Ukraine-Rus*.

**1914–1918**    Ukrainians serve in both the Russian and rival Austro-Hungarian armies during World War I. Ukraine becomes a battleground in the war, and tens of thousands of Ukrainians are killed.

**1917**    Revolution in Moscow forces Czar Nicholas II to give up the throne. A group of Ukrainians establishes a government in eastern Ukraine. But this new leadership proves unable to establish control of the country. Bolsheviks, led by Communist V. I. Lenin, eventually seize control of Russia.

**1918–1921**    Chaos reigns in Ukraine as a series of ineffective governments attempt to rule Ukraine. Meanwhile, the country serves as a battleground in the fight between the Bolsheviks and their enemies.

**1922**    Ukraine becomes the Ukrainian Soviet Socialist Republic and is incorporated into the new Union of Soviet Socialist Republics.

**LATE 1920s**    Soviet leader Joseph Stalin's attempts to collectivize Ukrainian farms lead to violent protest from Ukraine's peasants.

**1930–1932**    Stalin responds to Ukrainian resistance by causing a massive famine in the Ukraine. About 5 million Ukrainians die.

**1941**    Germany invades the Soviet Union in June 1941.

**1945**    Germany surrenders, ending World War II. By this time, about 5.3 million Ukrainans have died.

**1958**    After a five-year power struggle, Ukrainian Nikita Khrushchev emerges as the successor to Joseph Stalin.

**1970s**    The Soviet economy declines, and the Ukrainian standard of living plummets.

**1985**    In search of a remedy for the Soviet Union's problems, new Soviet leader Mikhail Gorbachev introduces the policies of glasnost (openness) and perestroika (restructuring).

**1986**    An explosion at the Chornobyl nuclear power plant spreads radioactive debris across a huge swath of Ukraine and Belarus. Government handling of the disaster causes widespread anger among the Ukrainian population.

**1991**    Ukraine claims its independence on August 24. The Soviet Union dissolves on December 25.

**1996**    Plagued by economic problems, the government introduces a new currency, the hryvnia.

**2003**    The Ukrainian government sends 1,600 Ukrainian troops to help stabilize the postwar situation in Iraq.

**2004**    Protesters flood the streets of Kyiv and other cities after Prime Minister Viktor Yanukovych is declared winner of a fraudulent election. Challenger Viktor Yushchenko is declared the winner in a rerun held on December 26.

**COUNTRY NAME** Ukraine

**AREA** 233,089 square miles (603,700 sq. km)

**MAIN LANDFORMS** Carpathian Mountains, Dnipro-Prypyat Lowlands, Northern Ukrainian Upland, Central Plateau, Coastal Plain, Crimean Peninsula

**HIGHEST POINT** Mount Hoverla, 6,762 feet (2,061 m)

**LOWEST POINT** Black Sea, sea level

**MAJOR RIVERS** Dnipro, Dnister, Donets, Prypyat, Southern Buh

**ANIMALS** carp, golden eagles, grouse, gulls, kingfishers, marmots, owls, partridges, perch, pike, red-capped woodpeckers, roe deer, short-toed eagles, sturgeon, wild pigs, wolves

**CAPITAL CITY** Kyiv

**OTHER MAJOR CITIES** Dnipropetrovsk, Donetsk, Kharkiv, Lviv, Odesa

**OFFICIAL LANGUAGE** Ukrainian

**MONETARY UNIT** Hryvnia. 100 kopiykas = 1 hryvnia

---

## UKRAINIAN CURRENCY

Ukraine's currency is the hryvnia (named after the coinage of the old kingdom of Kyivan Rus). Notes are printed in denominations of 1, 2, 5, 10, 20, 50, and 100. Coins are called kopiykas—or kopeks for short. The Ukrainian government began circulating hryvnia bills in 1996 to replace the *karbovanets*, a temporary currency that was created in 1992 to replace the Soviet ruble. (Many Ukrainians still refer to hryvnia notes as rubles.) Each colored note features an image of a famous Ukrainian on the face. An image of a famous building that is related to that person appears on the back. For example, the 2-hryvnia note features an image of Kyivan Rus ruler Yaroslav the Wise. The image on the back is of Kyiv's Saint Sofia Cathedral, which Yaroslav built.

Ukraine's flag is divided into two horizontal bands of equal width. The top band is azure (a light blue). The bottom is golden yellow. The top band is generally believed to represent the sky, while the bottom represents Ukraine's wheat or sunflowers. The Ukrainian flag was adopted on January 28, 1992.

The Ukrainian national anthem, "Ukraine Is Not Yet Dead," was first adopted during the brief period of Ukrainian independence in the early 1920s. It became the anthem of the newly independent Ukraine after the fall of the Soviet Union. Despite its somewhat gloomy title, the lyrics express hope and optimism about the country's future as a free nation. Below is a translation of the anthem's first verse.

### Ukraine Is Not Yet Dead
Ukraine's glory hasn't perished, nor her freedom
Upon us, fellow compatriots, fate shall smile once more.
Our enemies will vanish, like dew in the morning sun,
And we too shall rule, brothers, in a free land of our own.
We'll lay down our souls and bodies to attain our freedom,
And we'll show that we, brothers, are of the Kozak nation.

For a link where you can listen to the Ukrainian national anthem, go to www.vgsbooks.com.

**ISAAC BABEL** (1894–1941) One of Ukraine's greatest writers, Babel was born in Moldavanka, a Jewish ghetto suburb of Odesa. His most famous work, *Odesa Tales,* is a collection of vivid short stories about Jews in his hometown. He also wrote about his service in the Russian military during World War I. Babel was one of the most famous and celebrated authors during the 1930s but was purged under Stalin late in that decade. He died in a Soviet prison camp in 1941.

**OKSANA BAIUL** (b. 1977) Baiul captured the world's attention—and a gold medal—with her brilliant figure skating routines at the 1994 Winter Olympics in Lillehammer, Norway. Born in Dnipropetrovsk, Baiul won her first competition at the age of seven. After the 1994 games, she turned professional and moved to the United States. Since then Baiul has performed on many figure skating tours and also designs her own line of figure skating apparel.

**PETER BONDRA** (b. 1968) Bondra is one of the National Hockey League's most exciting players. The speedy right-winger won league scoring titles in 1995 and 1998. He is the Washington Capitals' all-time leader in points (825), goals (472), power-play goals (137), game-winning goals (73), shorthanded goals (32) and hat tricks (19). Bondra was traded to the Ottawa Senators in 2004. He was born in Lutsk in northwestern Ukraine.

**ROALD HOFFMANN** (b. 1937) Hoffmann was awarded the 1981 Nobel Prize in Chemistry for his groundbreaking work in the study of chemical reactions. Born into a Jewish family in Zloczow, Poland (later Zloczew, Ukraine), Hoffmann and his family were imprisoned in a German concentration camp during the early years of World War II. He and his mother escaped and were sheltered by a Ukrainian family. His father was killed. Hoffmann moved to the United States in 1949. He studied at Columbia University and Harvard and performed much of his research at Cornell University. Hoffmann also writes poetry.

**VLADIMIR HOROWITZ** (1903–1989) Horowitz, one of the most celebrated concert pianists of the twentieth century, was born in Berdychev in west central Ukraine. Displaying a great musical gift at a young age, he moved to Kyiv at the age of twelve to hone his craft. By his early twenties, he had become one of the most famous pianists in Europe, known for his brilliant performances of the works of Chopin, Liszt, Rachmaninoff, Prokofiev, and others. Horowitz settled in the United States in 1940.

**MYKHAILO HRUSHEVSKY** (1866–1934) Ukraine's most distinguished historian was born in Kholm in modern-day Poland. He studied at Kyiv University, specializing in Ukrainian history and literature. In 1898 Hrushevsky published the first volume of his ten-volume

*History of Ukraine-Rus,* a groundbreaking work that helped to define Ukraine's identity as a nation. A political activist, he was elected president of the first of the short-lived Ukrainian governments that emerged during and after the Russian Revolution.

**BOHDAN KHMELNYTSKY** (ca.1595–1657) The greatest of the Cossack hetmans was born in Chyhyryn in western Ukraine. A member of the Polish szlachta, or landowning class, Khmelnytsky was forced to flee his home after a dispute with his local governor. Taking refuge in the Zaporozhian Sich, he soon came to be its leader. In 1648 he led the Cossacks in a massive uprising against Polish rule. After suffering defeat in battle, he turned to the Russians for aid and signed an agreement that eventually led to Russian rule of the region.

**NIKITA KHRUSHCHEV** (1894–1971) Born to a poor peasant family in Kalynivka, a village near the Russian-Ukrainian border, Khrushchev succeeded Joseph Stalin as the leader of the USSR in the 1950s. Khrushchev encouraged "peaceful coexistence" with the West. But he also pushed the Soviet Union into competition with the United States in the building of larger and more powerful nuclear weapons and in the race to achieve goals in space.

**THE KLITSCHKO BROTHERS** Vitali (b. 1971) and Wladimir (b. 1975) Klitschko are both fearsome heavyweight boxers. Each holds several championship belts. Both are also highly educated, having earned doctorate degrees in physical science and sports. The sons of a Soviet air force colonel, Vitali was born in Belovodsk, Kyrgyzstan. Wladimir was born in Semipalatinsk (Kazakhstan).

**YANA KLOTCHKOVA** (b. 1982) Born in the Crimean city of Symferopol, Klotchkova is one of Ukraine's most popular athletes and the best female all-around swimmer in the world. At the 2000 Summer Olympic Games in Sydney, Klotchkova won gold medals in both the 200- and 400-meter individual medley events, as well as a silver medal in the 800-meter medley. She repeated her gold medal heroics at the 2004 games in Athens, Greece.

**TARAS SHEVCHENKO** (1814–1861) Ukraine's greatest poet and national hero was born into a poor serf family in Moryntsi in western Ukraine in 1814. Shevchenko showed such a gift for sketching and painting that he earned a place at the Academy of Arts in the Russian capital of Saint Petersburg. He published his first collection of poems, *Kobzar,* in 1840, earning widespread acclaim. Shevchenko's writings about Ukrainian history and Cossack legends made him a leader in the Ukrainian nationalist movement. For this, Russian authorities arrested him in 1847. He spent ten years in a Siberian prison camp. When released, he resumed writing but died a few years later.

**CARPATHIAN NATURAL NATIONAL PARK** Cutting through Ukraine's western tip, the Carpathian Mountains are the country's most picturesque region and the best place to see Ukraine's natural wonders. The 194-square-mile (503 sq. km) Carpathian Natural National Park was declared a protected area in 1980. The park's many trails make it one of the country's best places for hikers, and its steep, snowy slopes are a popular spot for skiers.

**KYIV** Ukraine's capital has a rich and storied history. The dazzling Saint Sofia Cathedral is arguably Kyiv's most popular attraction. The structure, built in the eleventh century, features stunning gold domes and a lavishly painted exterior. The inside of the building includes stunning frescoes (paintings made on freshly plastered walls) as well as the marble tomb of the great Kyivan ruler, Yaroslav the Wise. The Caves Monastery, located on the banks of the Dnipro, features gold-domed churches, historic museums, and a series of winding underground caves lined with mummified Orthodox Christian monks. Khreshchatyk, Kyiv's elegant commercial boulevard, is a busy area full of a wide variety of shops and a perfect place for people watching.

**LVIV** The cultural center of western Ukraine is home to many unique sights. Much of Lviv has been recently restored after decades of Communist neglect. One of the few major Ukrainian cities to escape major damage during World War II, Lviv boasts a wide variety of architecture, from the ornate baroque style of Saint George Cathedral to the breathtaking neoclassical design of the Ivan Franko Theater of Opera and Ballet. The city's museums include the Lviv Historical Museum, which traces the city's rich history; and the Lviv Museum of Ethnography and Handicrafts, which features exhibits of stunning Ukrainian handicrafts.

**ODESA** This seaport city is often referred to as the "Pearl of the Black Sea" and is home to a unique mix of nationalities and cultures. Highlights for any visitor include walks along the chestnut-tree-lined, seaside promenade and climbing the 192 Potemkin Steps that connect the harbor to the city. Visitors can explore the seemingly endless network of catacombs that lie below the city's surface or relax on Odesa's crowded sandy beaches. A wide variety of museums and art galleries are also open to tourists.

**YALTA** This elegant Crimean resort city was once a favorite summer residence for Russian royalty. In modern times, Yalta remains a top tourist attraction. Set between the Black Sea and the picturesque Crimean Mountains, the city enjoys pleasant weather year-round. While Yalta's sandy beaches are its main attraction, the city is also home to a variety of museums, cathedrals, and parks. Young visitors will enjoy the Polyana Skazok (Fairy-Tale Glade), an open-air museum featuring statues of characters from Ukrainian and Russian children's stories.

**chornozem:** a rich, fertile, black soil present throughout much of the Ukrainian steppes

**collective farm:** a large agricultural estate worked by a group. The workers usually received a portion of the farm's harvest as wages. On a Soviet collective farm, the central government owned the land, buildings, and machinery.

**Commonwealth of Independent States:** a union of eleven former Soviet Republics that was created by the leaders of Russia, Belarus, and Ukraine in December 1991

**Communist:** a person who supports Communism, an economic system in which the government owns all farmland and the means of producing goods in factories

**Cossack:** a member of a military brotherhood that was first organized by former serfs. The Cossacks lived in the lower Dnipro River valley and fought the rulers of Russia and Poland for Ukrainian independence.

**coup d'état:** French words meaning "blow to the state" that refer to a swift, sudden overthrow of a government

**ethnic Russian:** a person whose ethnic heritage is Slavic and who speaks Russian

**ethnic Ukrainian:** a person whose ethnic heritage is Slavic and who speaks Ukrainian

**free-market economy:** a system that allows the free exchange of goods at prices determined by supply and demand

**glasnost:** a Russian word meaning "openness" that refers to a policy of easing restrictions on writing and speech

**hetman:** one of the elected leaders of the Cossacks

**peasant:** a small landowner or landless farmworker

**perestroika:** a policy of economic restructuring introduced in the late 1980s that loosened Soviet control of industry and agriculture

**Russian Empire:** a large kingdom that covered present-day Russia as well as areas to the west and south. It existed from roughly the mid-1500s to 1917.

**Russify:** to make Russian by imposing the Russian language and culture on non-Russian peoples

**serf:** a rural worker under the feudal landowning system, which tied laborers to a farming estate for life. Serfs had few rights and owed their labor and a large portion of their harvest to the landowner.

**Slav:** a member of an ethnic group that originated in central Asia and later moved into Russia, Ukraine, and eastern Europe

**steppe:** a flat, treeless plain that stretches across central, northern, and eastern Ukraine

**Glossary**

**Selected Bibliography**

**Ascherson, Neal.** *Black Sea.* **New York: Hill and Wang, 1995.**
This book is a lively and engaging study of the Black Sea and the rich history that surrounds it.

*BBC* **(British Broadcasting Corporation)** *News Online.* **2005.**
http://news.bbc.co.uk/2/hi/europe/default.stm **(January 13, 2005)**
The BBC's Europe section is a helpful resource for news on Ukraine and other European nations.

**Central Intelligence Agency (CIA). 2005.**
http://cia.gov/cia/publications/factbook/geos/up.html **(February 8, 2005)**
The "World Factbook" section of the CIA's website contains basic information on Ukraine's geography, people, economy, government, communications, transportation, military, and transnational issues.

**Conquest, Robert.** *The Harvest of Sorrow: Soviet Collectivization and the Terror-Famine.* **New York: Oxford University Press, 1984.**
This powerful book, written by a leading historian of the Soviet Union, chronicles the Soviet collectivization drive and subsequent terror-famine that killed and displaced millions of Ukrainians in the late 1920s and early 1930s.

**Dalton, Meredith.** *Culture Shock! Ukraine: A Guide to Customs and Etiquette.* **Portland, OR: Graphic Arts Publishing Company, 2001.**
This volume in the Culture Shock! series explores Ukraine's culture, customs, and traditions.

*The Economist.* **2005.**
http://www.economist.com **(February 8, 2005)**
Both the website and print edition of this British newspaper provide up-to-date coverage of Ukrainian news and events.

**Hamm, Michael F.** *Kiev: A Portrait, 1800–1917.* **Princeton, NJ: Princeton University Press, 1993.**
Written by an American history professor, this book studies the unique history of the Ukrainian capital during the nineteenth century up to the Russian Revolution.

**Hodges, Linda, and George Chumak.** *Language and Travel Guide to Ukraine.* **3rd ed. New York: Hippocrene Books, 2000.**
Filled with useful facts about Ukraine's history, religion, arts, literature, and customs, this book also features a very useful guide to the Ukrainian language.

**Magosci, Paul Robert.** *A History of Ukraine.* **Seattle: University of Washington Press, 1996.**
This comprehensive study, written by one of the top scholars on the subject, covers Ukrainian history from prehistoric times to independence and beyond.

**Population Reference Bureau. 2005.**
http://www.prb.org/ **(January 13, 2005)**
The annual statistics on this site provide a wealth of data on Ukrainian population, birthrates and death rates, the fertility rate, the infant mortality rate, and other useful demographic information.

**Reid, Anna. *Borderland: A Journey through the History of Ukraine.* Boulder, CO: Westview Press, 2000.**
In this book, a British journalist explores the history of Ukraine through several of the country's unique regions.

**Savage, Ania. *Return to Ukraine.* College Station: Texas A&M University Press, 2000.**
In this vivid study, Ukrainian-American journalist Ania Savage weaves Ukrainian history with her own personal account of returning to Ukraine following independence.

**Shoemaker, M. Wesley. *Russia and the Commonwealth of Independent States 2002.* 33rd ed. Harpers Ferry, WV: Stryker-Post Publications, 2002.**
The World Today series' volume on Russia and the Commonwealth of Independent States includes a chapter that explores the land, people, history, and culture of Ukraine.

**Subtleny, Orest. *Ukraine: A History.* 3rd ed. Toronto: University of Toronto Press, 2000.**
This thorough study, written by one of the world's foremost scholars of Ukraine, covers the history of the country from its very earliest times to the present.

**Wilson, Andrew. *The Ukrainians: Unexpected Nation.* New Haven, CT: Yale University Press, 2000.**
Written by a historian from the University College London, this book explores the history of Ukraine from the era of Kyivan Rus to post-Soviet independence.

**Bassis, Volodymyr.** *Ukraine.* **Tarrytown, NY: Marshall Cavendish, 1997.**
The Ukraine volume of the Cultures of the World series provides information on Ukraine's land, history, people, culture, and economy.

**Berkmoes, Ryan Ver, et al.** *Russia, Ukraine & Belarus.* **2nd ed. Oakland: Lonely Planet Publications, 2000.**
This handy guide to the three European former Soviet states provides a wealth of information on Ukraine's history, people, and customs, as well as information on the best places to stay and visit and how to reach them.

**Dowswell, Paul.** *The Chernobyl Disaster, April 26, 1986.* **Chicago: Raintree, 2003.**
The volume in the Days that Shook the World series explores the events of the Chornobyl nuclear power plant explosion and the Soviet government's handling of the crisis.

**Dupont, Lonnie Hull.** *Oksana Baiul.* **Broomall, PA: Chelsea House Publications (1998).**
Learn more about the Ukrainian figure skating legend from this biography.

**Goldstein, Margaret J.** *World War II—Europe.* **Minneapolis: Lerner Publications Company, 2004.**
This volume from Lerner's Chronicles of America's Wars series covers World War II in Europe, including the epic struggle between Germany and the Soviet Union.

**Hesse, Karen.** *Letters from Rifka.* **New York: Hyperion Books for Children, 1993.**
This novel tells the story of Rifka, a young Ukrainian Jewish girl, who escapes her homeland during the Russian Civil War in 1919. Fleeing war and persecution, Rifka finally finds her way to safety in the United States.

**Kallen, Stuart A., and Rosemary Wallner.** *The Khrushchev Era, 1953–1965.* **Edina, MN: Abdo Publishing Company, 1992.**
This volume in the Rise and Fall of the Soviet Union series covers the period when Ukrainian-born Nikita Khrushchev served as leader of the Soviet Union.

**Kummer, Patricia.** *Ukraine.* **New York: Children's Press, 2000.**
The Enchantment of the World Series' volume on Ukraine features information on the land, history, economy, culture, and people of Ukraine.

*Kyiv Post*
http://kyivpost.com/
The web edition of the *Kyiv Post* newspaper features news and opinion covering current events in Ukraine.

**Márquez, Herón.** *Russia in Pictures.* **Minneapolis: Lerner Publications Company, 2004.**
Learn more about the geo75graphy, history, people, culture, and economy of Ukraine's neighbor and former fellow member of the Soviet Union.

Further Reading and Websites

**Otfinoski, Steven. *Ukraine.* New York: Facts on File, Inc., 1999.**
This volume in the Nations in Transition series provides a useful summary of basic information about Ukraine.

**Sherman, Josepha. *The Cold War.* Minneapolis: Lerner Publications Company, 2004.**
Learn more about the Cold War, a conflict that pitted the Soviet Union against the United States for nearly fifty years, in this book from the Chronicle of America's War series.

**Stalcup, Ann. *Ukrainian Egg Decoration: A Holiday Tradition.* New York: PowerKids Press, 1999.**
This book discusses Ukraine's unique Easter egg decorating tradition and even includes step-by-step instructions for how to create your own pysanky.

**Ukrainian Congress Committee of America**
http://www.ucca.org/
The Ukrainian Congress Committee of America is an organization that represents the interests of ethnic Ukrainians living in the United States. The organization's website features news and current events from Ukraine and information about Ukrainians living in the United States.

**Ukrainian World Congress**
http://ukrainianworldcongress.org/info/index.shtml
The Ukrainian World Congress website features information about Ukrainians living around the world and numerous facts and statistics about Ukraine.

**vgsbooks.com**
http://www.vgsbooks.com
Visit vgsbooks.com, the homepage of the Visual Geography Series®. You can get linked to all sorts of useful on-line information, including geographical, historical, demographic, cultural, and economic websites. The vgsbooks.com site is a great resource for late-breaking news and statistics.

**Welcome to Ukraine**
http://www.wumag.kiev.ua/
This companion website to *Welcome to Ukraine* magazine features information on the country, many articles on various Ukrainian subjects, and numerous stunning photos.

**Captions for photos appearing on cover and chapter openers:**

Cover: A wealthy German businessman had this 1912 villa, called the Swallow's Nest, built in Yalta in the style of a French castle. Under Soviet rule, many well-to-do Russians and Europeans enjoyed vacationing on Ukraine's Black Sea coast.

pp. 4–5 A young supporter of opposition candidate Viktor Yushchenko waves a Ukrainian flag at a rally in Kyiv's Independence Square to protest the results of the presidential elections held on November 21, 2004. Yushchenko's rival, Prime Minister Viktor Yanukovych, was declared the winner, but reports of widespread voter fraud brought thousands of protesters to the streets. This event has come to be known as the Orange Revolution after the orange colors of Yushchenko's party.

pp. 8–9 The Prut River winds through Ukraine's Carpathian Mountains. The river flows near the southeastern border between Ukraine and Romania.

pp. 36–37 Crowds look at goods at an open-air market on Andryivsky Street in Kyiv.

pp. 44–45 An ornately dressed group of Orthodox clergy, including the patriarch of Ukraine *(center)*, enters Saint Michael's Cathedral in Kyiv.

pp. 56–57 Golden wheat fields blanket the landscape in southern Ukraine.

**Photo Acknowledgments**
The images in this book are reproduced courtesy of: © VASILY FEDOSENKO/Reuters/CORBIS, pp. 4–5, 35 (right); Dr. Anatol and Mrs. Daria Lysyj, pp. 8–9, 34, 39, 58; © Martin Barlow/Art Directors, pp. 12, 59; © Patrick Johns/CORBIS SYGMA, p. 13; © Kostin Igor/CORBIS, p. 14; © Sergey Pozharsky/Art Directors, p. 16; © Matthew Turner/Art Directors, p. 17; © Sinan Anadol/Atlas Geographic, pp. 20, 36–37; © Michael Nicholson/ CORBIS, p. 24; © Brown Brothers, p. 25; Library of Congress, pp. 26, 30 (LC- USZW33-024195-C); © Hulton Archive/Getty Images, p. 27; The Ukrainian Museum, p. 28; The Illustrated London News and Picture Library, p. 29; Dwight D. Eisenhower Library, p. 32; © Chris Niedenthal/Time Life Pictures/Getty Images, p. 33; © GLEB GARANICH/Reuters/CORBIS, p. 35 (left); © Jeff Greenberg/Art Directors, p. 40; Natalia Lysyj Rieland, pp. 43, 44–45, 48; © Eugene G. Schulz, pp. 46, 54 (top); © Michael O'Brien/Art Directors, p. 47; © Dimitri Mossienko/Art Directors, pp. 50, 62; © Tibor Bognar/Art Directors, p. 53; © Reuters/CORBIS, p. 54 (bottom); © Stephane Reix/For Picture/CORBIS, p. 55; © Warren Jacobs/Art Directors, pp. 56–57; © V. Slapinia/Art Directors, p. 61; © Trip/Art Directors, p. 63; AP/Wide World Photos, p. 65; © Todd Strand/Independent Picture Service, p. 68; Laura Westlund, p. 69.

Front Cover: © Ernest Manewal/SuperStock; Back Cover: NASA